Camille Corot: 175 Paintings, Drawings and Etchings

Paintings&Drawings, Volume 11

Maria Tsaneva

Published by Icon-m, 2014.

Camille Corot: 175 Paintings, Drawings and Etchings

By Maria Tsaneva

First Edition
Copyright © 2013 by Maria Tsaneva

Camille Corot: 175 Paintings, Drawings and Etchings

Also by Maria Tsaneva

Paintings&Drawings
Artemisia Gentileschi: 52 Masterpieces
Camille Corot: 175 Paintings, Drawings
and Etchings

Foreword

Jean-Baptiste-Camille Corot (1796 - 1875) was a French landscape painter and printmaker in etching. He was the leading painter of the Barbizon school of France in the mid-nineteenth century. Corot is a pivotal figure in landscape painting and his vast output simultaneously references the Neo-Classical tradition and anticipates the plein-air innovations of Impressionism. Of him Claude Monet exclaimed "There is only one master here—Corot. We are nothing compared to him, nothing."

Corot often credited as a precursor of Impressionist practice, but he approached his landscapes more traditionally than is usually believed. Compared to the Impressionists who came later, Corot's palette is restrained, dominated with browns and blacks ("forbidden colors" among the Impressionists) along with dark and silvery green. Though appearing at times to be rapid and spontaneous, usually his strokes were controlled and careful, and his compositions well-thought out and generally rendered as simply and concisely as possible, heightening the poetic effect of the imagery. As he stated, "I noticed that everything that was done correctly on the first attempt was more true, and the forms more beautiful."

His contributions to figure painting are hardly less important; Degas preferred his figures to his landscapes, and the classical figures of Picasso pay overt homage to Corot's influence. Corot produced a number of prized figure pictures. While the subjects were sometimes placed in pastoral settings, these were mostly studio pieces, drawn from the live model with both specificity and subtlety. Like his landscapes, they are characterized by a contemplative lyricism, with his late paintings L'Algérienne

(Algerian Woman) and La Jeune Grecque (The Greek Girl) being fine examples.

Corot painted about fifty portraits, mostly of family and friends. He also painted thirteen reclining nudes, with his Les Repos (1860) strikingly similar in pose to Ingres famous Le Grande Odalisque (1814), but his female is instead a rustic bacchante. In perhaps his last figure painting, "Lady in Blue" (1874), Corot achieves an effect reminiscent of Degas, soft yet expressive. In all cases of his figure painting, the color is restrained and is remarkable for its strength and purity.

Corot also executed many etchings and pencil sketches. Some of the sketches used a system of visual symbols—circles representing areas of light and squares representing shadow. He also experimented with the cliché verre process—a hybrid of photography and engraving. Starting in the 1830s, Corot also painted decorative panels and walls in the homes of friends, aided by his students.

Corot's early training, from 1822 onwards, was with the classicising landscape painters Michallon and Bertin, and in 1825 he went to Italy, via Switzerland, for two years. He spent most of his time in and around Rome, where he developed, through painting on the spot, his sensitive treatment of light, form and distance in terms of tonal values rather than by colour and drawing. In this he resembled Georges Michel (whom he knew), but never to the point of abandoning, for works to be exhibited, the traditional classical or religious subject; this he used as a disguise for his unconventional vision, although these carefully composed landscapes have little of the spontaneity of his sketches from nature.

He travelled widely in France 1827-34, and returned to Italy for several months in 1834 and 1843, his journeys being recorded in his drawings or his 'pochades,' which are small and very freely handled, and remarkable for the justness of their tonal values and the freshness of their colour.

By the early 1850s the tide of official and public favour had turned, possibly because by then he had developed for his Salon exhibits a fuzzy, woolly, poeticising manner entirely different from the directness and keenness of observation found in his sketches. This muzzy treatment of the landscape and trees in soft, grey-green tones became immensely popular, and has assured him the most notoriously prolific of all posthumous productions (it has been said that Corot painted 1,000 pictures, of which 1,500 are in America).

His very late figure studies and portraits are entirely free from the blurred and formless approach of his public manner, and show that in his 70s he was able to absorb the ideas of younger men, such as Courbet and Manet. His personal prestige with the younger generation was very great, and he did all in his admittedly limited power to soften the rigours of the Salon jury towards the works of unacademic artists.

He was a man of great simplicity and generosity and extremely charitable, as witness his support of Daumier in his blindness, Millet's widow, and his benefactions during the Franco-Prussian War.

There are examples of his art - autograph or attributed - in almost every museum of any size all over the world (there are 60 in the National Gallery, London, alone).

Corot summed up his approach to art around 1860 in this way: "I interpret with my art as much as with my eye."

Paintings

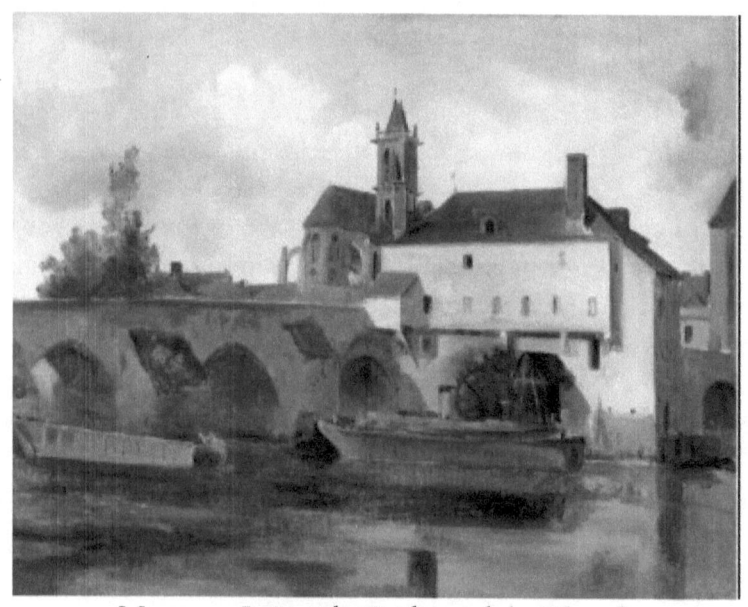

Moret sur Loing, the Bridge and the Church
1822, oil on canvas

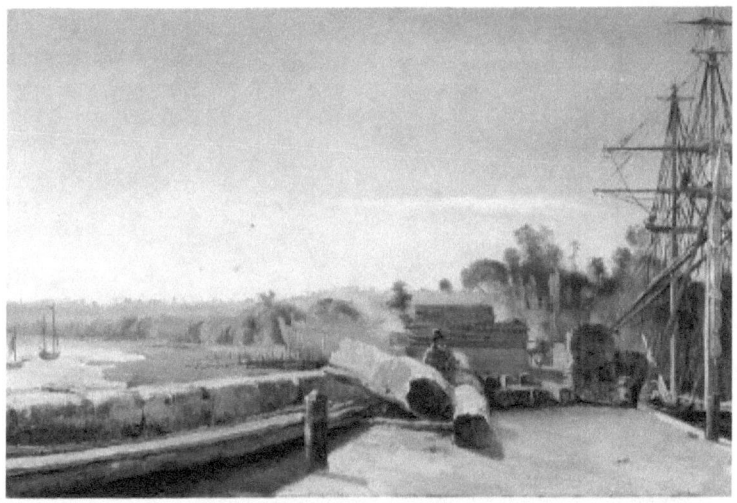

Shipyard in Honfleur
1823, oil on canvas

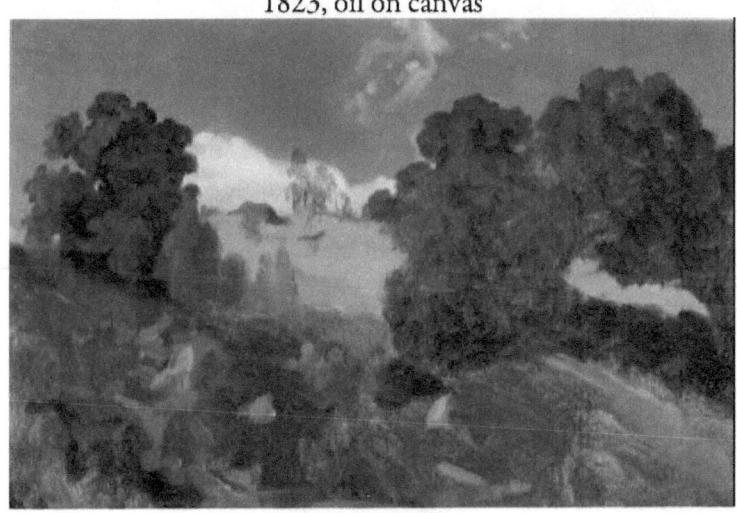

Fontainebleau
1823-24, oil on canvas

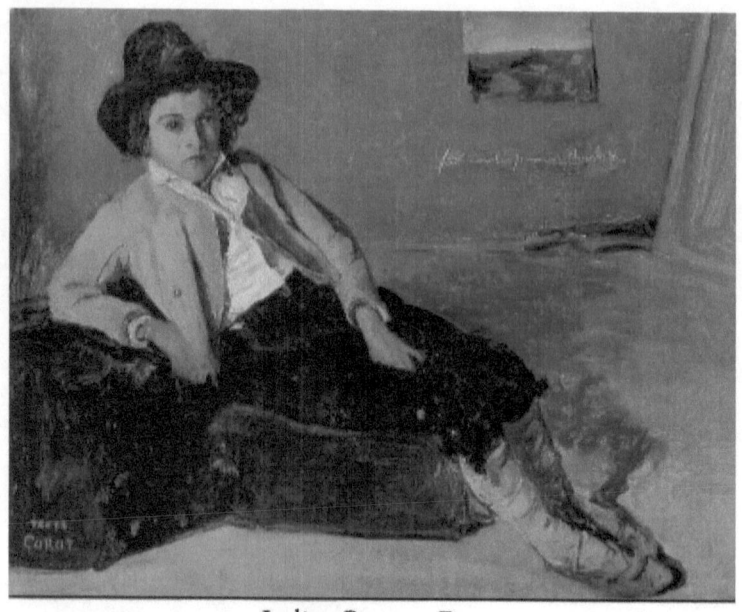

Italian Peasant Boy
1825, oil on canvas

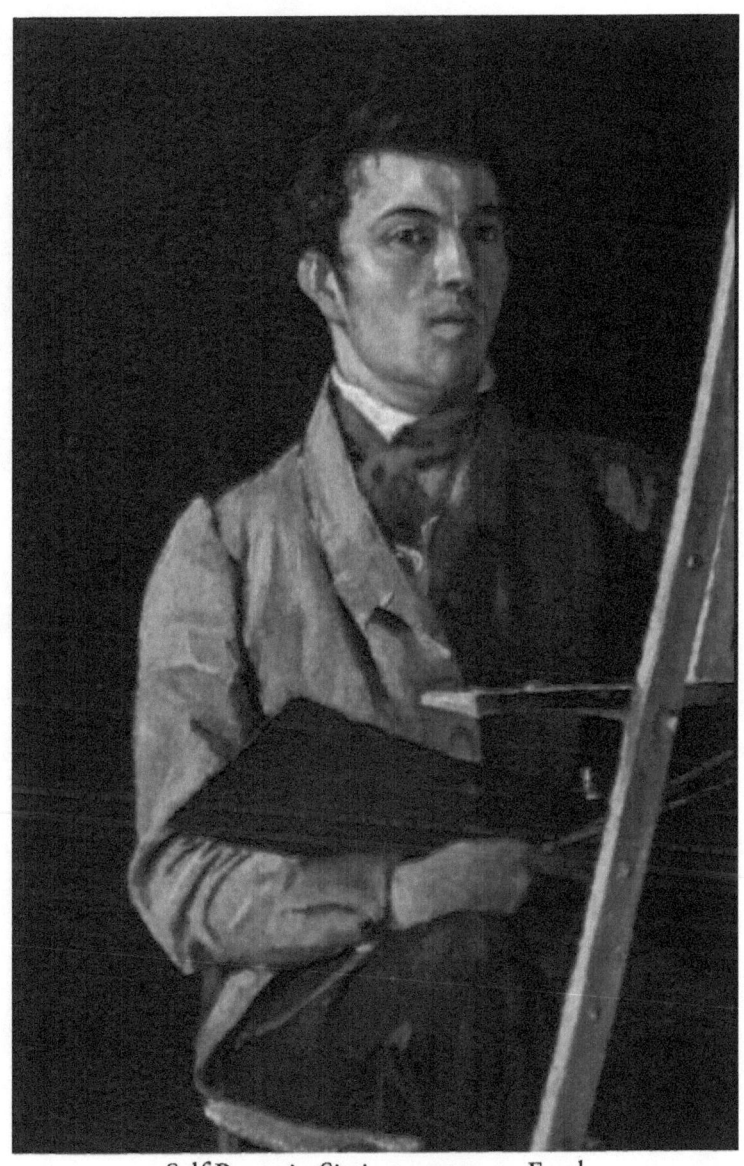

Self Portrait, Sitting next to an Easel
1825, oil on canvas

Maria Tsaneva

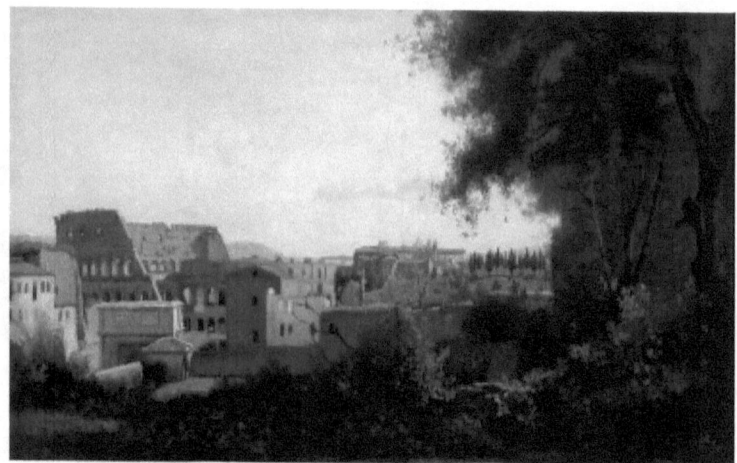

The Coliseum Seen from the Farnese Gardens
1826, Paper mounted on canvas

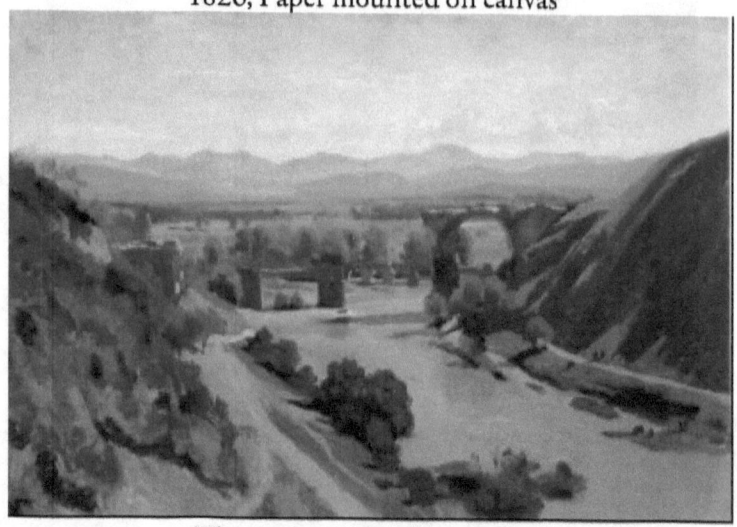

The Augustan Bridge at Narni
1826, oil on canvas

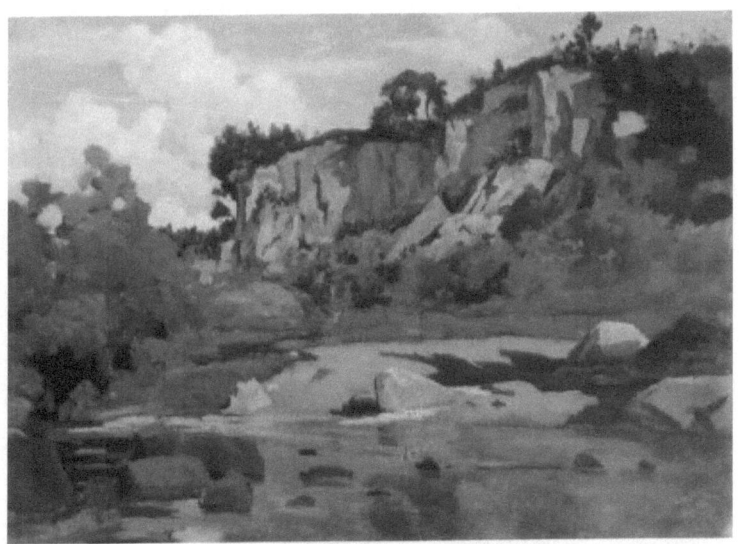

Civita Castellana
1826-27, oil on canvas

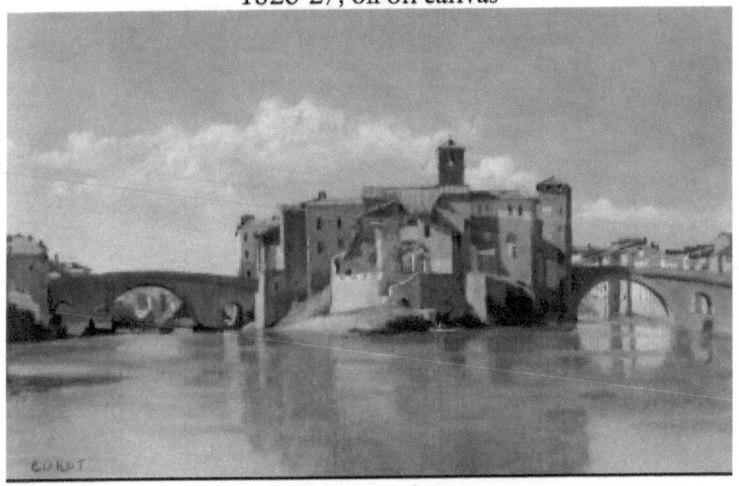

Rome, the Basilica of Constantine
1826-27, oil on canvas

Maria Tsaneva

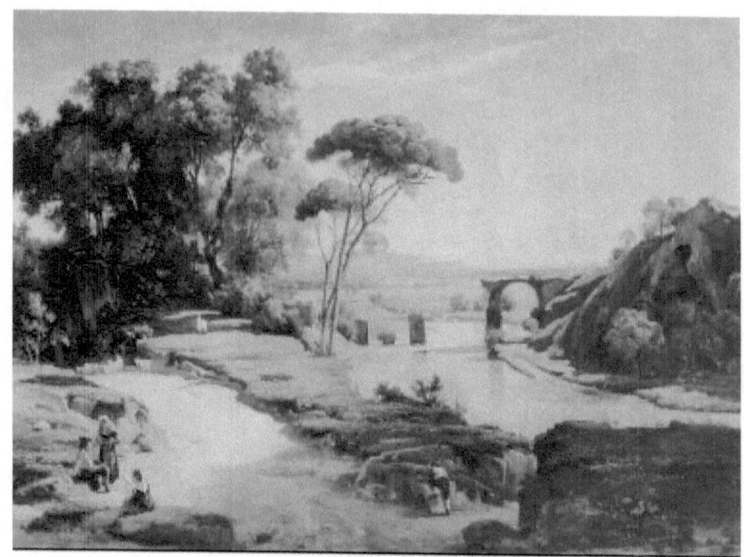

The Pont de Narni
1826-27, oil on canvas

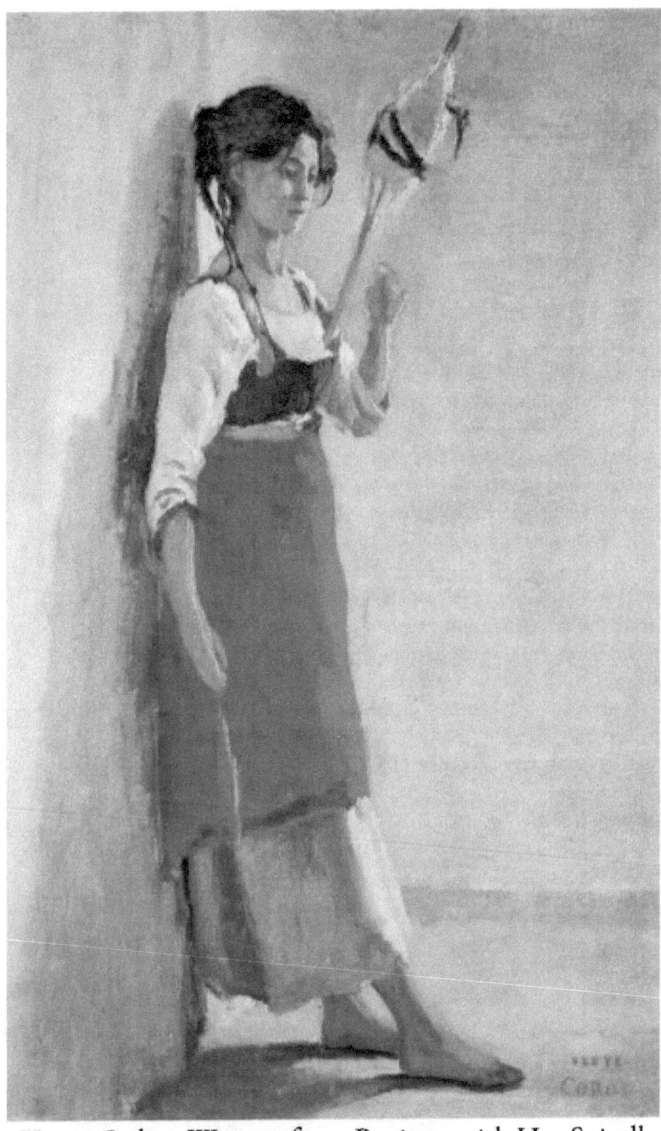

Young Italian Woman from Papigno with Her Spindl
1826-27, oil on canvas

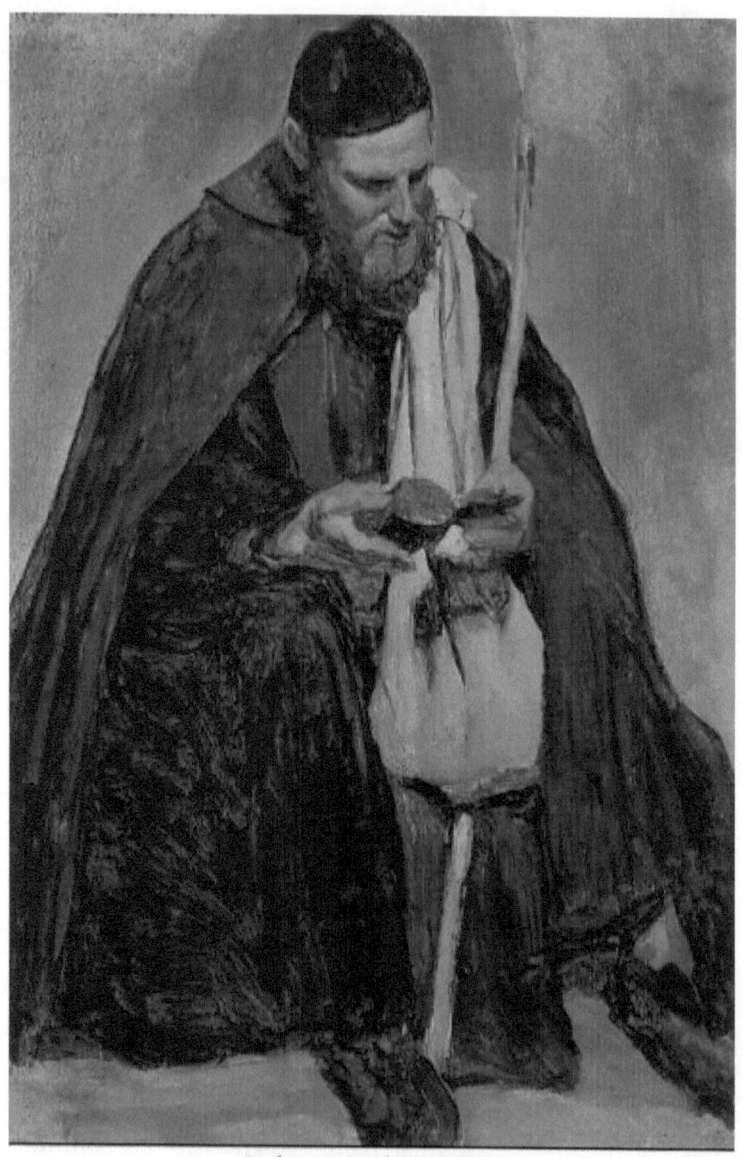

Italian Monk Reading
1826-28, oil on canvas

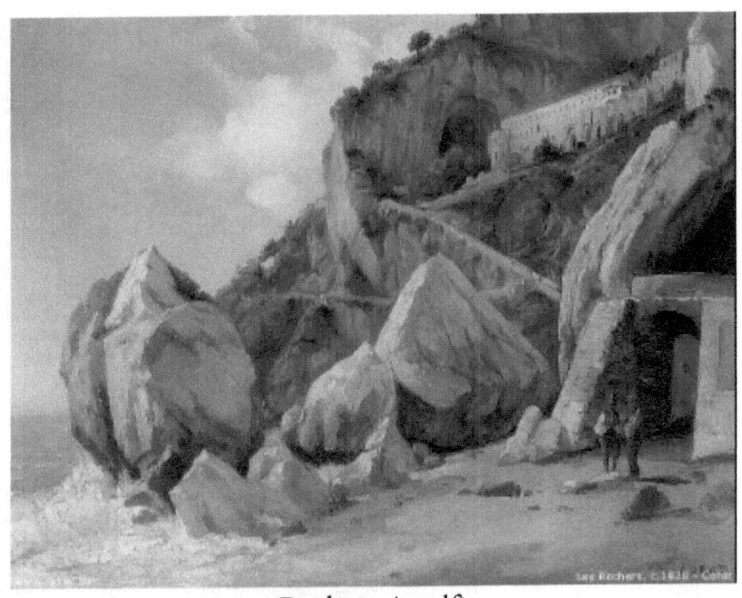

Rocks in Amalfi
1828, oil on canvas

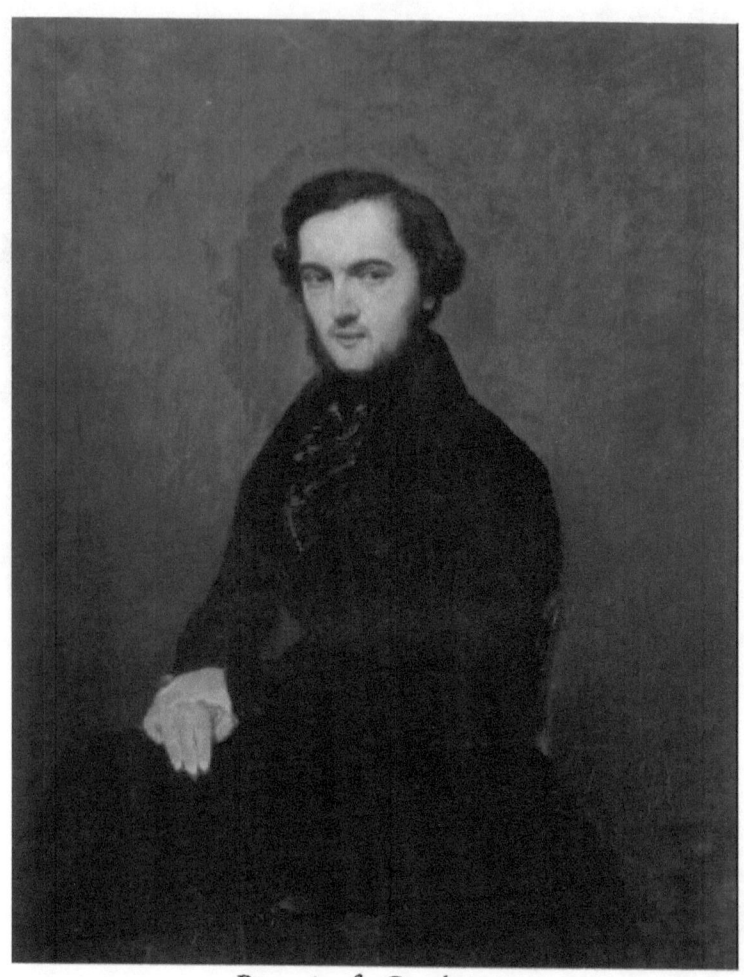

Portrait of a Gentleman
1829, oil on canvas

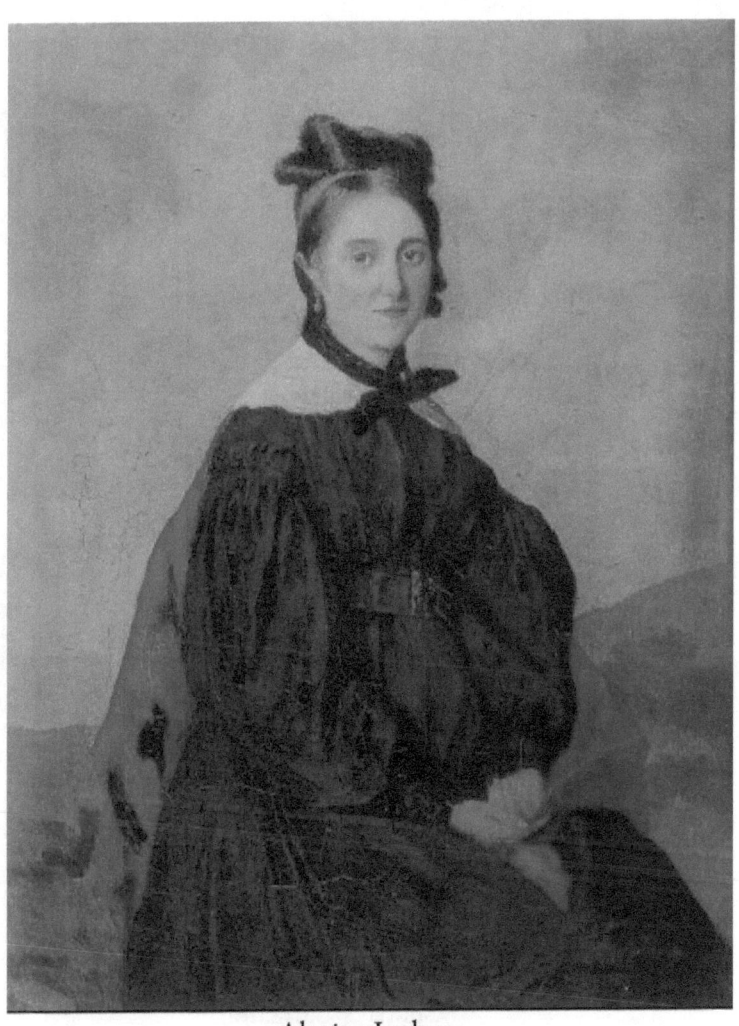

Alexina Ledoux
1830, oil on canvas

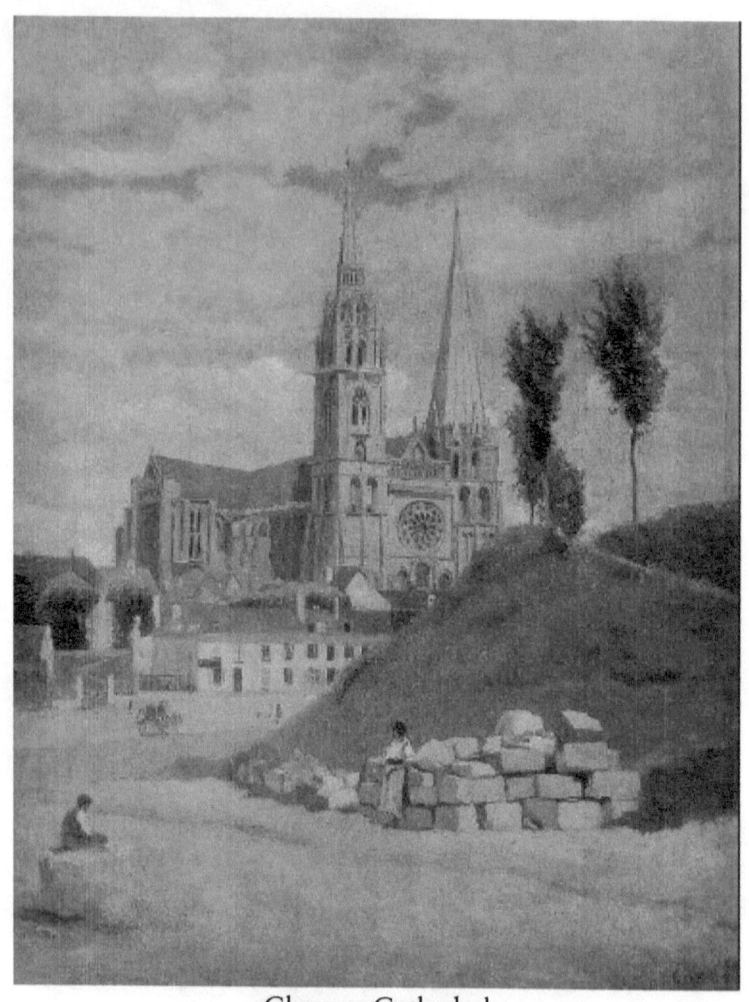

Chartres Cathedral
1830, oil on canvas

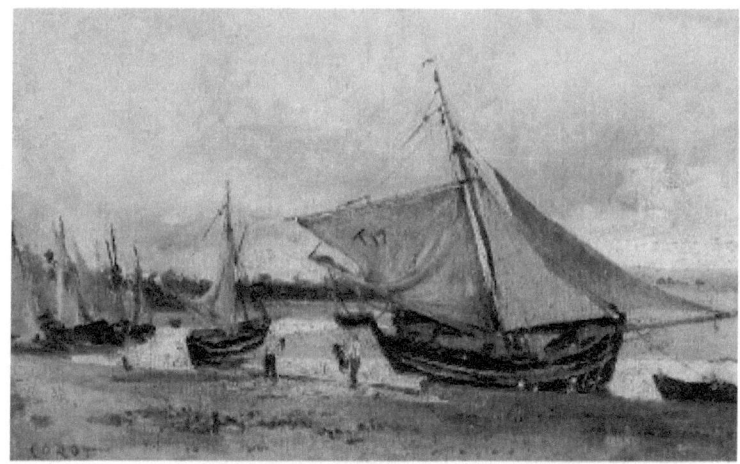

Fishing Boars Beached in the Chanel
1830, oil on canvas

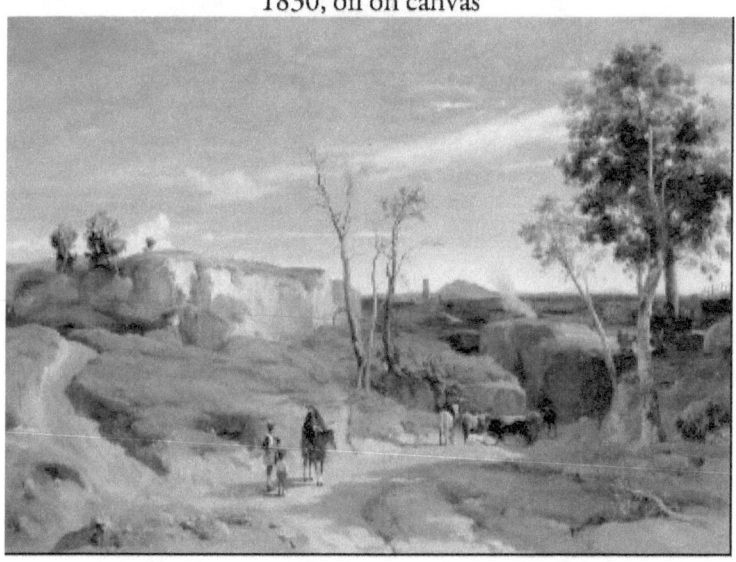

La Cervara, the Roman Countryside
1831, oil on canvas

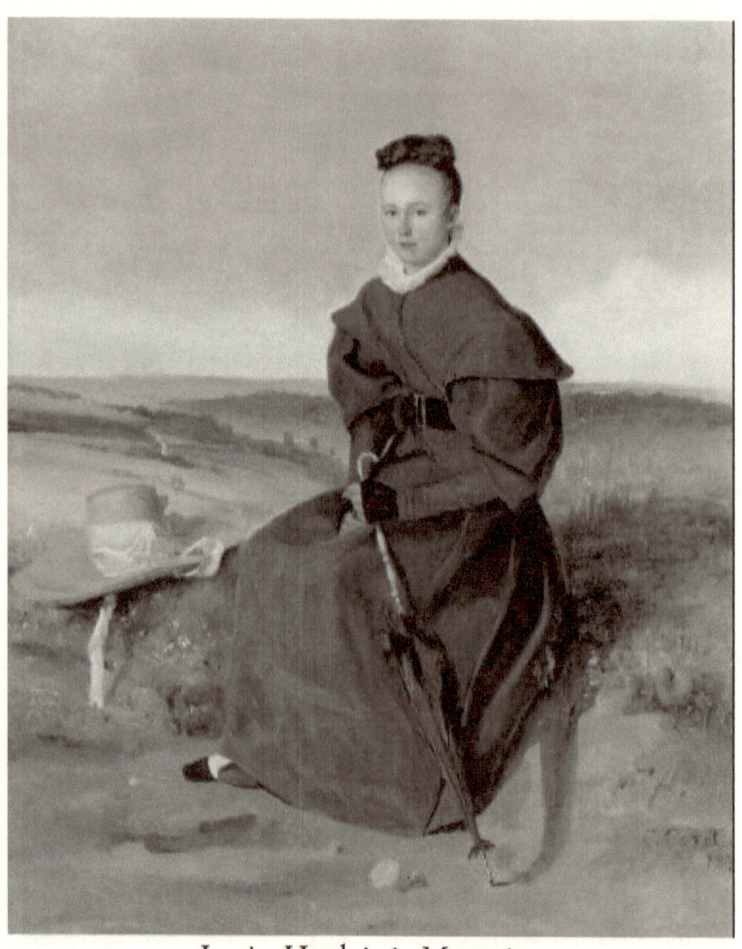

Louise Harduin in Mourning
1831, oil on canvas

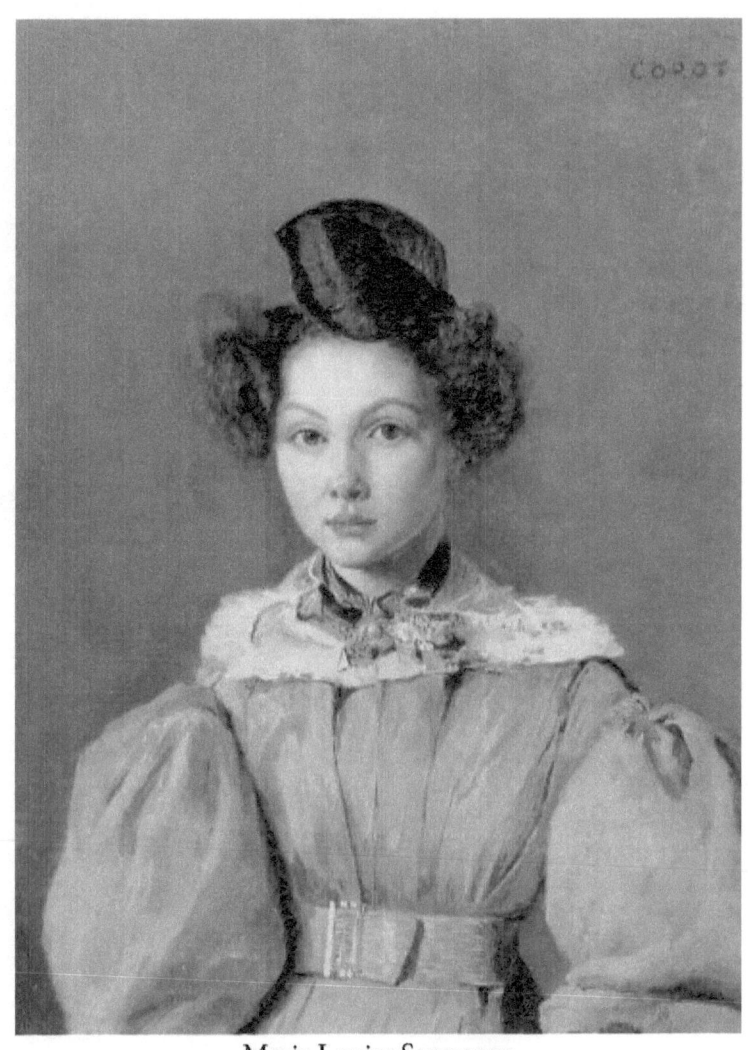

Marie Louise Sennegon
1831, oil on canvas

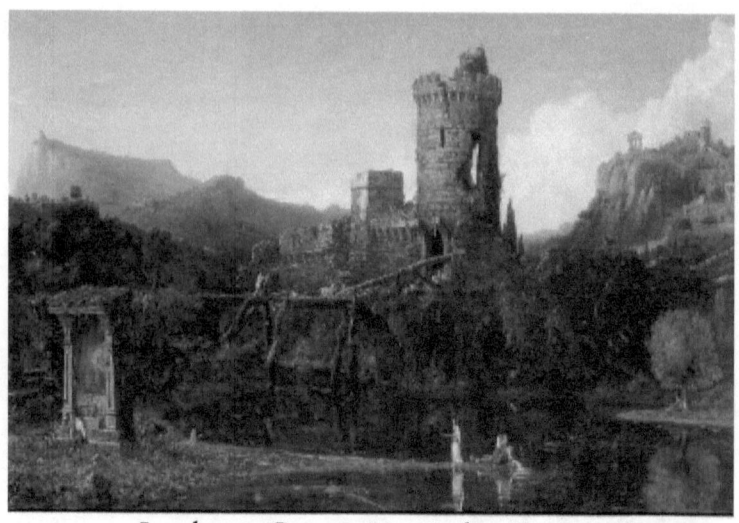

Landscape Composition Italian Scenery
1831-32, oil on canvas

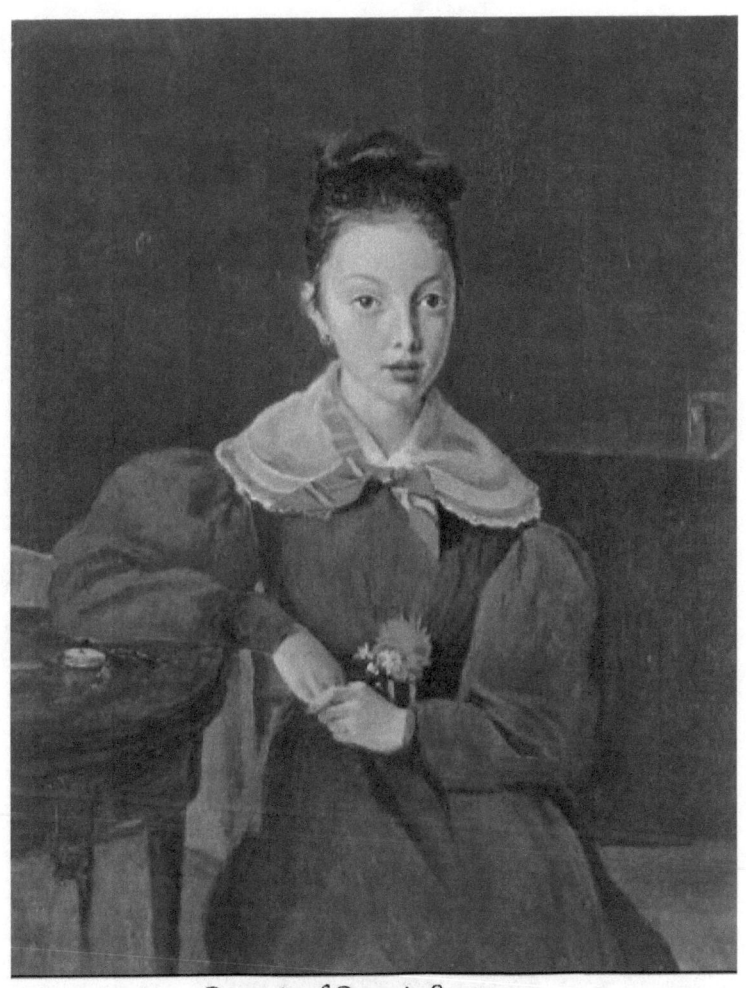

Portrait of Octavie Sennegon
1833, oil on canvas

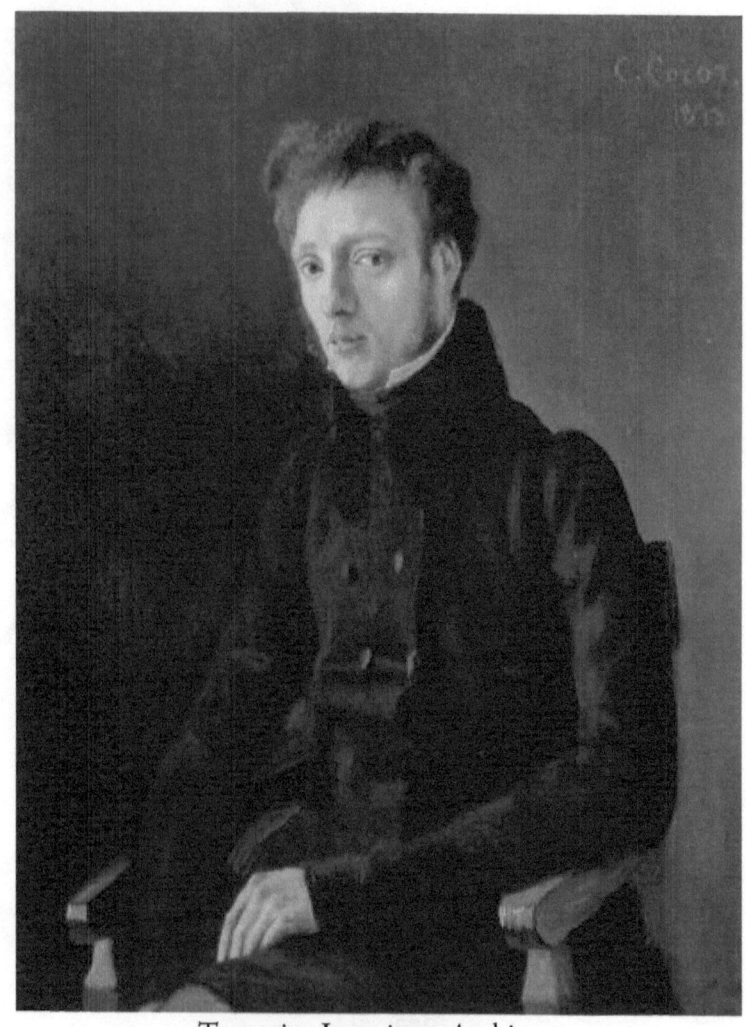

Toussaint Lemaistre, Architect
1833, oil on canvas

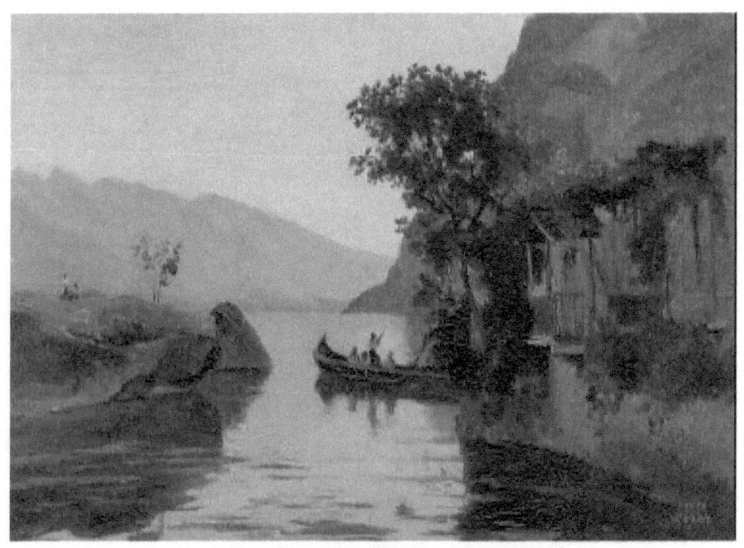

View at Riva, Italian Tyrol
1834, oil on canvas

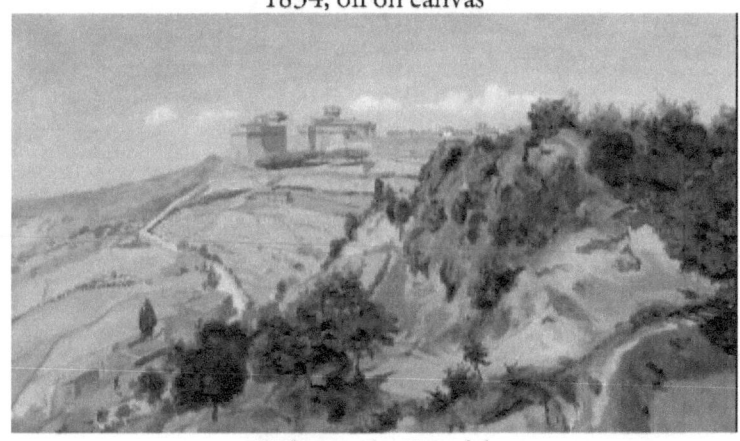

Voltarra the Citadel
1834, oil on canvas

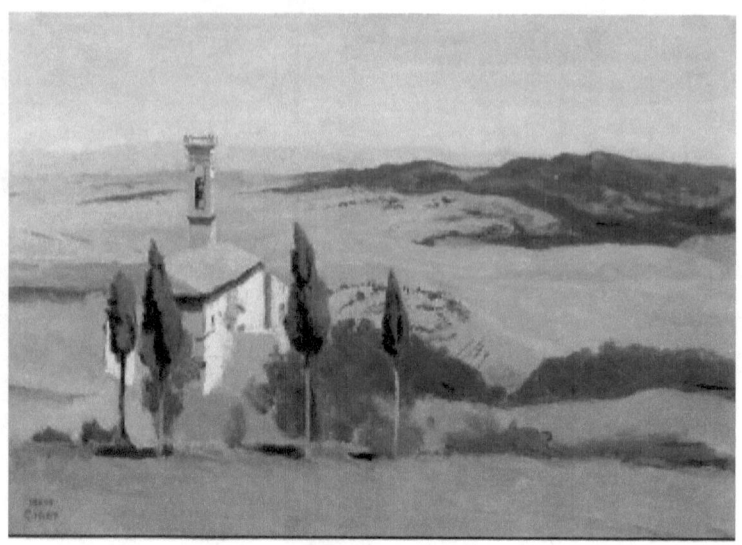

Volterra, Church and Bell Tower
1834, oil on canvas

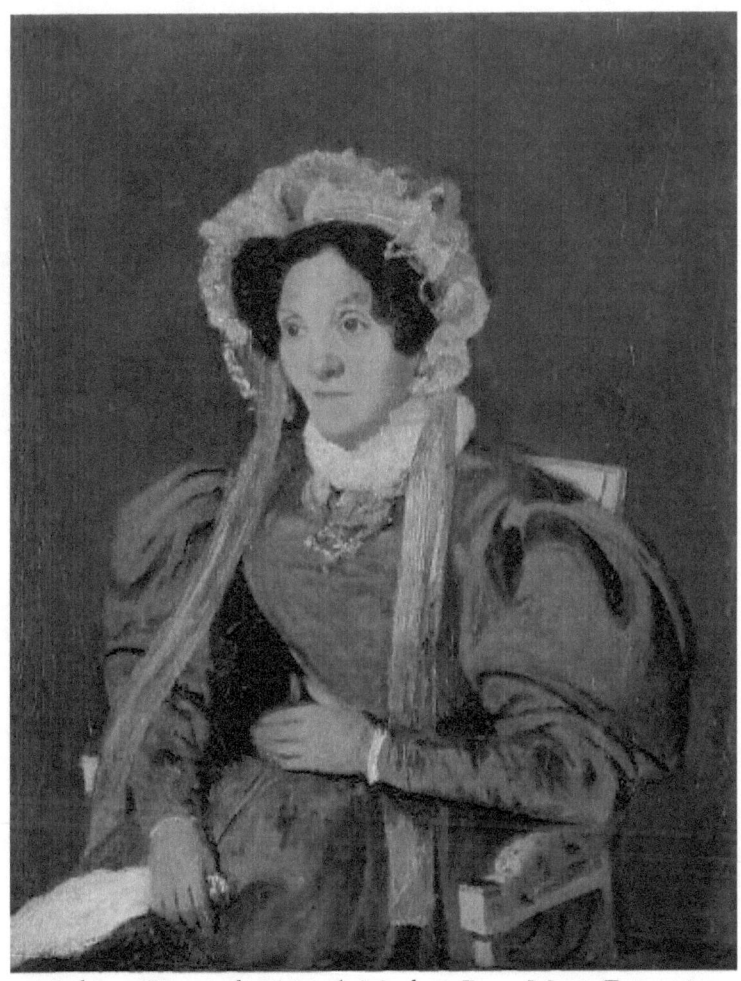

Madame Corot, the Artist's Mother, Born Marie Francoise
Oberson
1834-35, oil on canvas

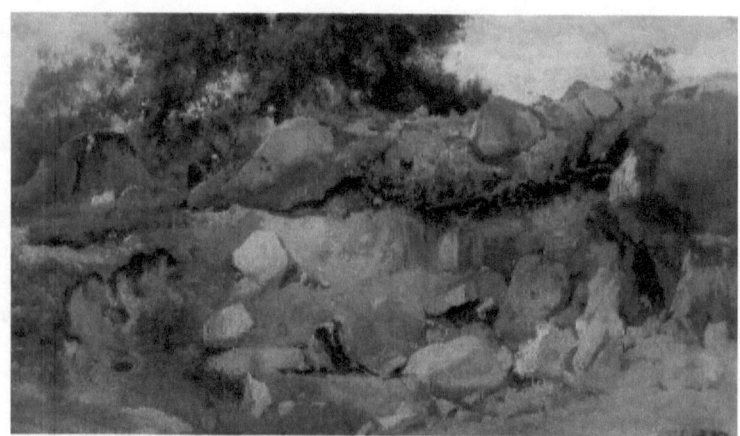

Quarry of the Chaise Mre at Fontainebleau
1835, oil on canvas

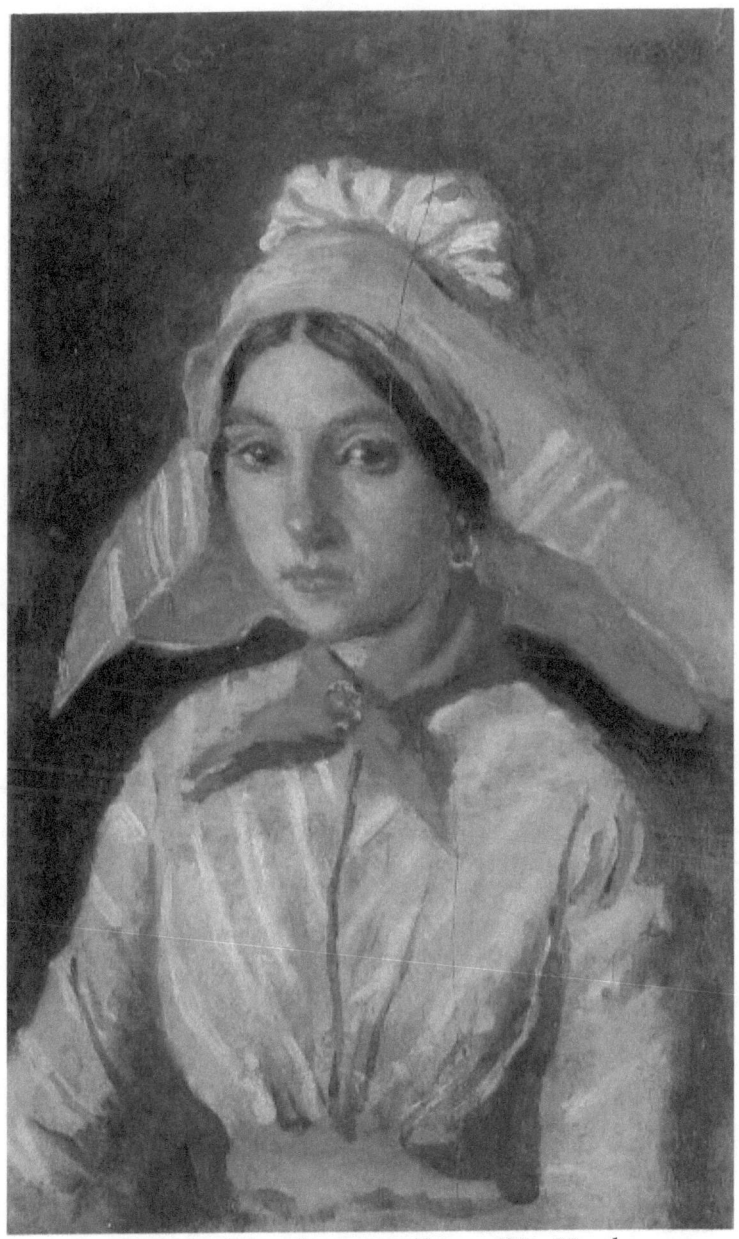

Young Girl with a Large Cap on Her Head
1835, oil on canvas

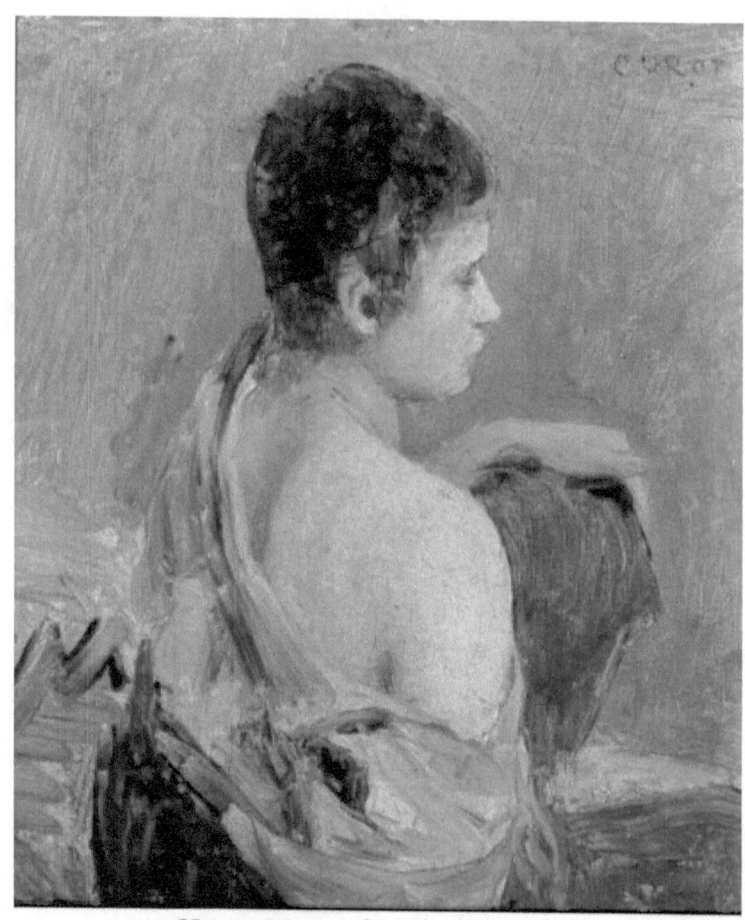

Young Man with Naked Shoulder
1835, oil on canvas

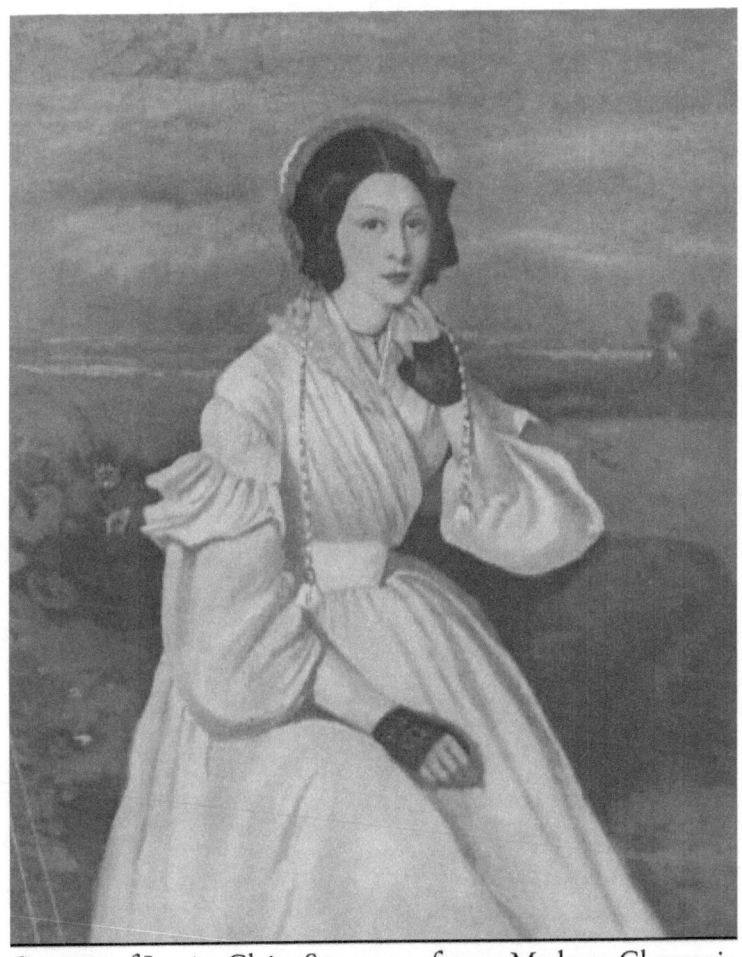

Portrait of Louise Claire Sennegon, future Madame Charmois
1837, oil on canvas

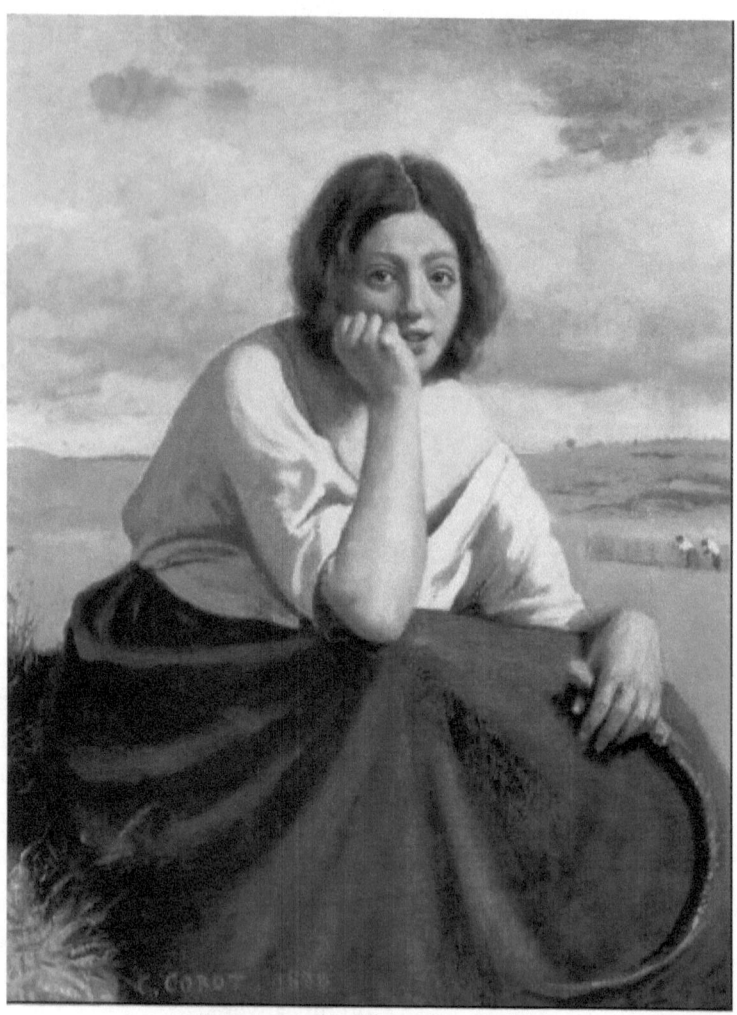

Harvester Holding Her Sickle
1838, oil on canvas

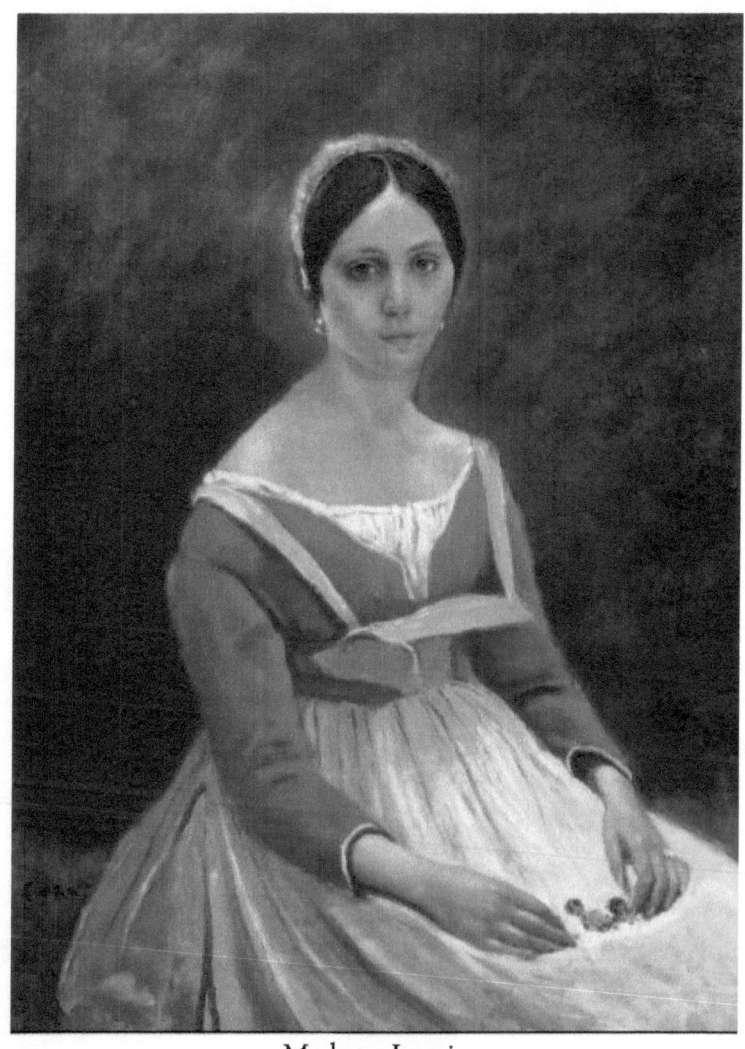

Madame Legois
1838, oil on canvas

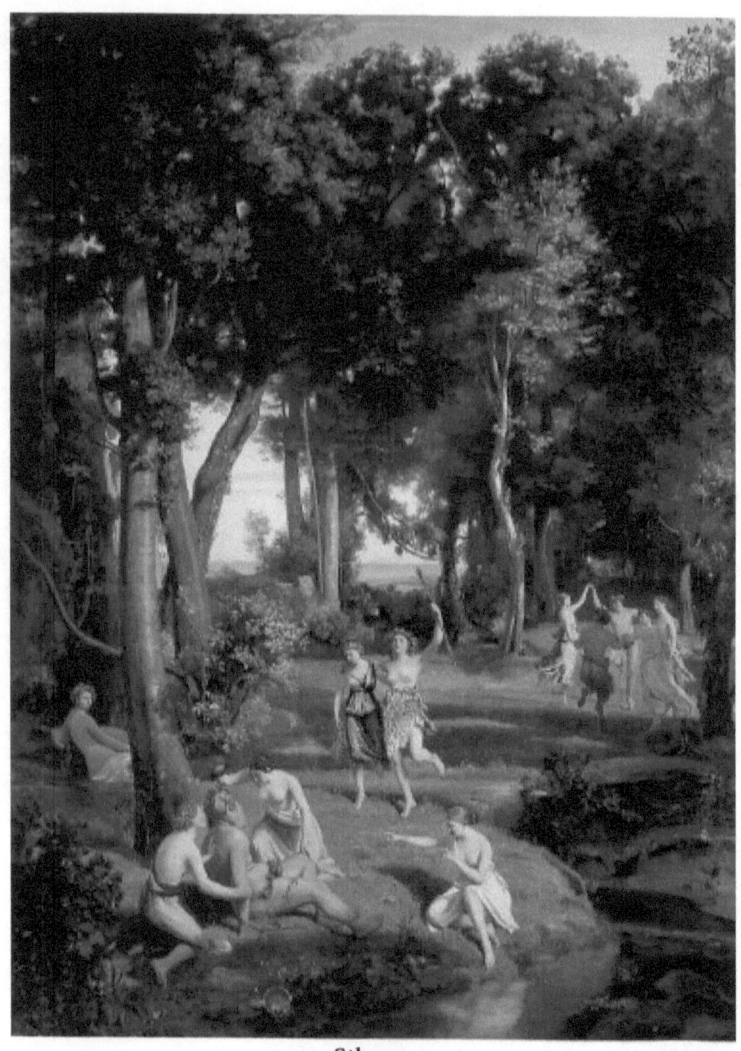

Silenus
1838, oil on canvas

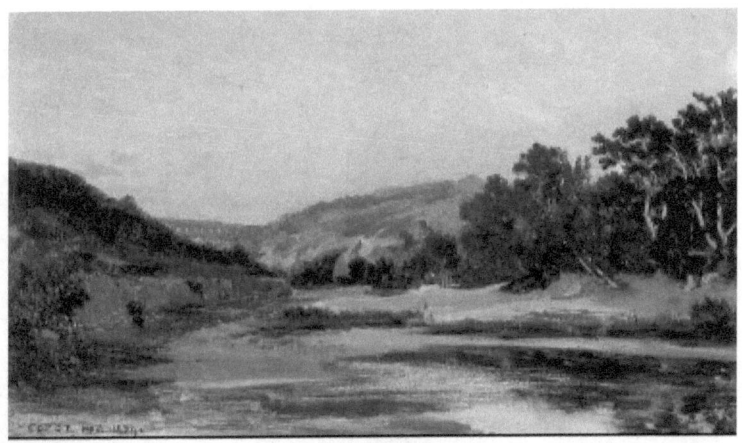

Aqueduct
1839, oil on canvas

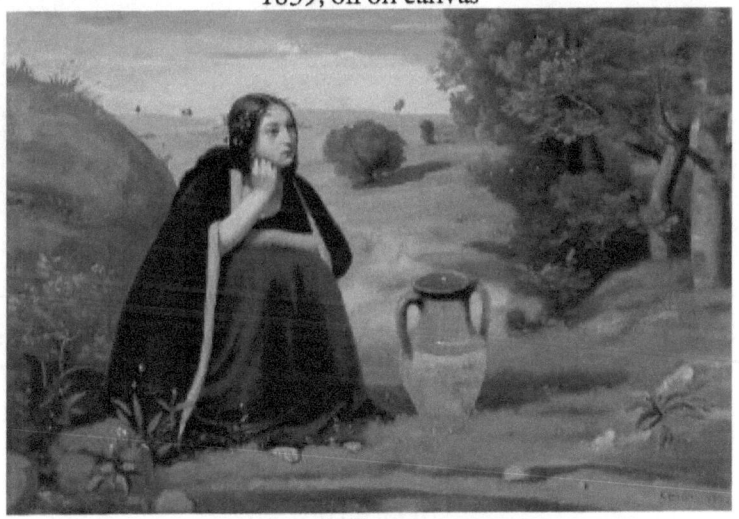

Rebecca
1839, oil on canvas

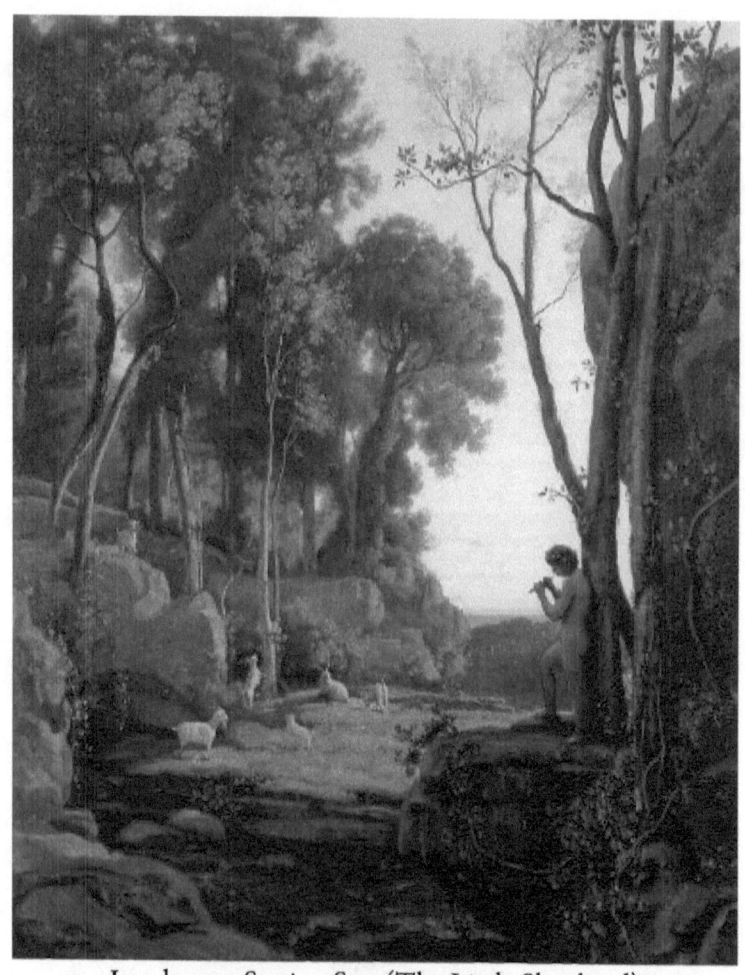

Landscape, Setting Sun (The Little Shepherd)
1840, oil on canvas

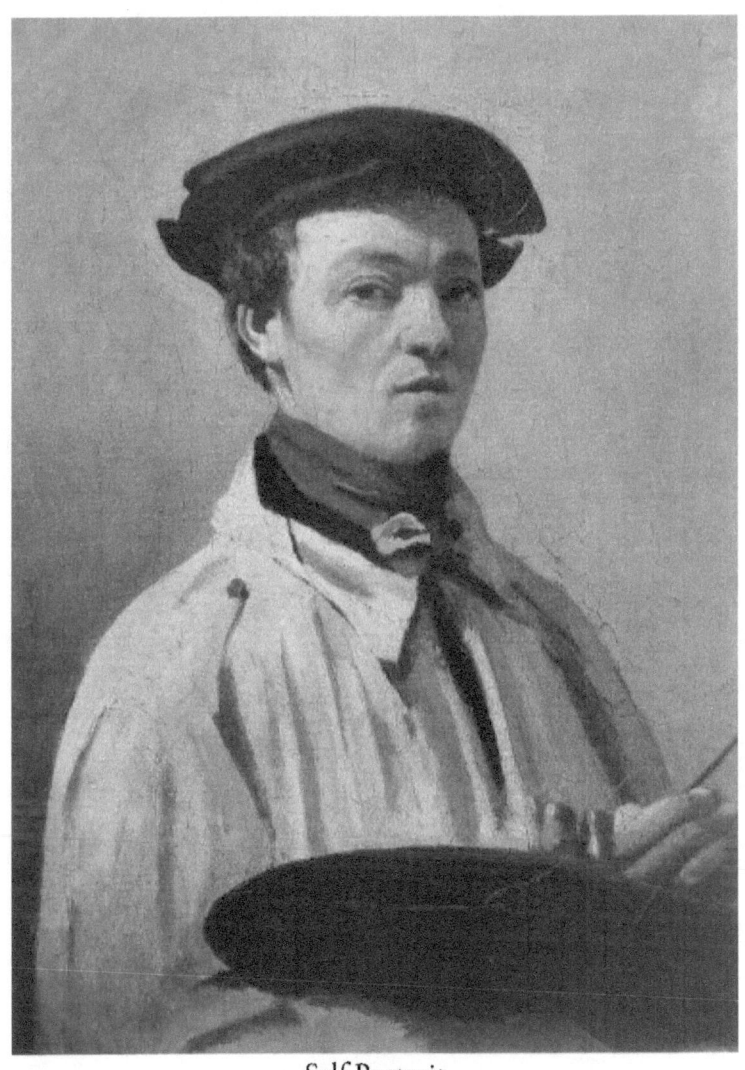

Self Portrait
1840, oil on canvas

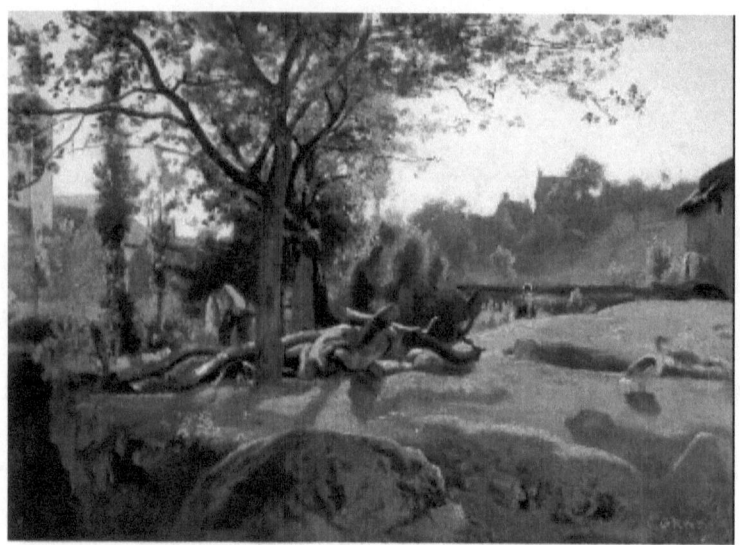

Peasants under the Trees at Dawn
1840-45, oil on canvas

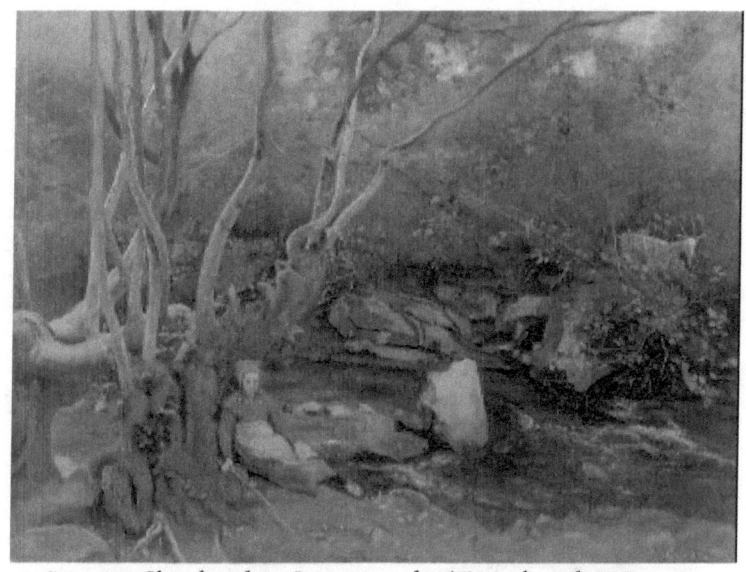

Lormes Shepherdess Sitting under Trees beside a Stream
1842, oil on canvas

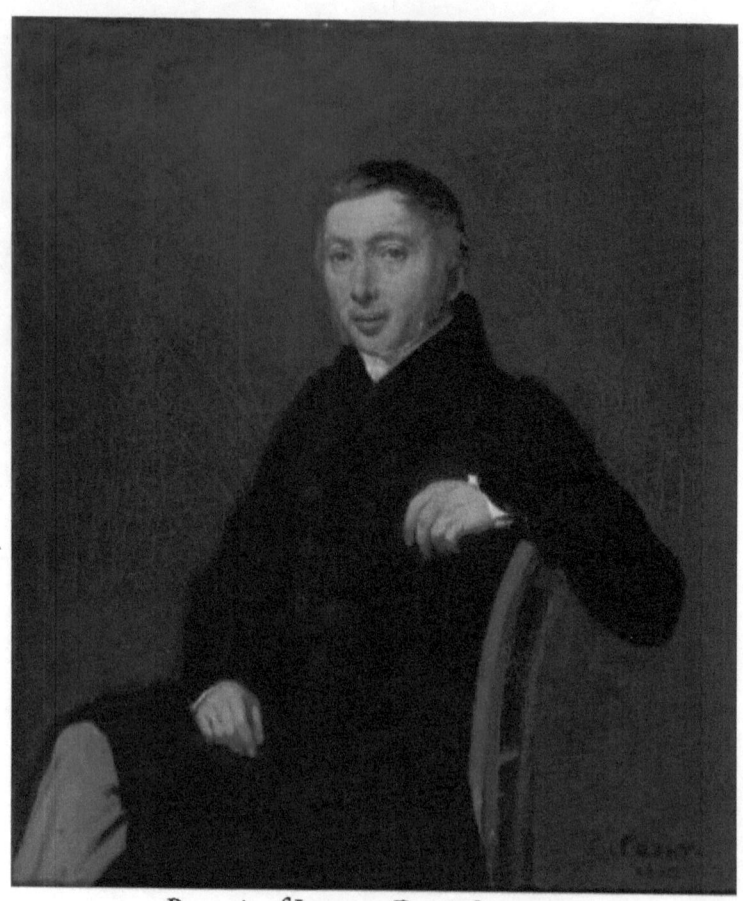

Portrait of Laurent Denis Sennegon
1842, oil on canvas

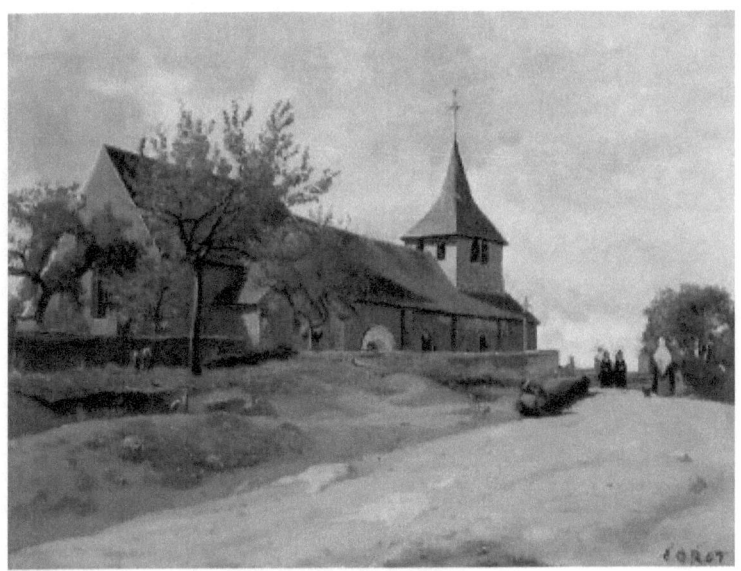

The Church at Lormes
1842, oil on canvas

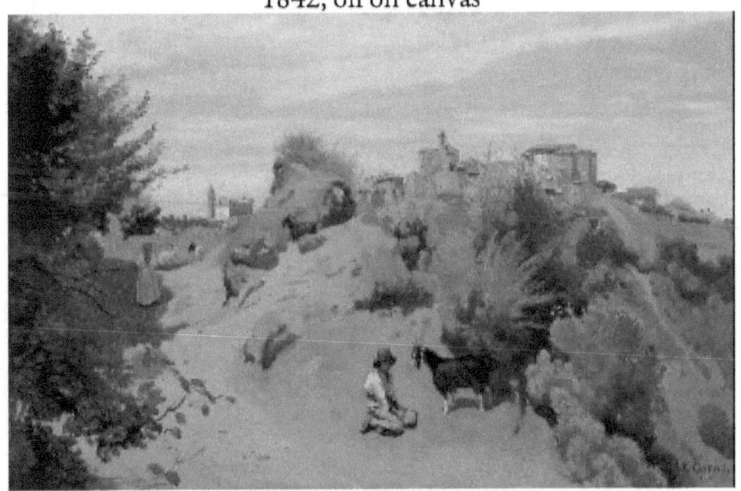

The goat herd of Genzano
1843, oil on canvas

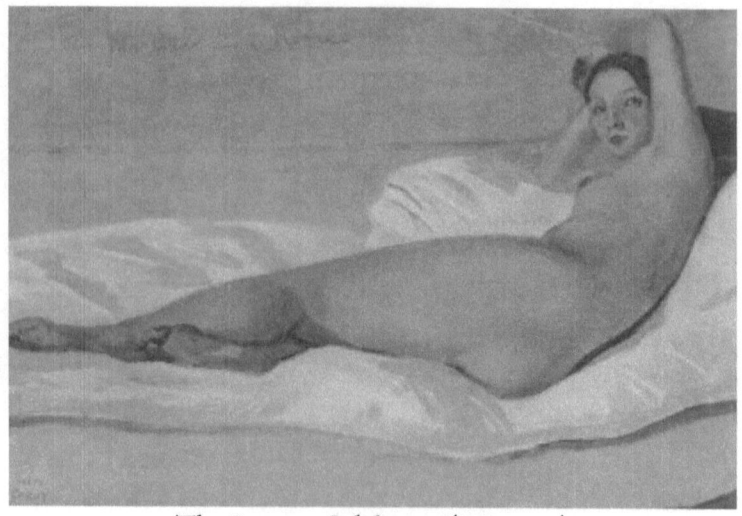

The Roman Odalisque (Marietta)
1843, oil on canvas

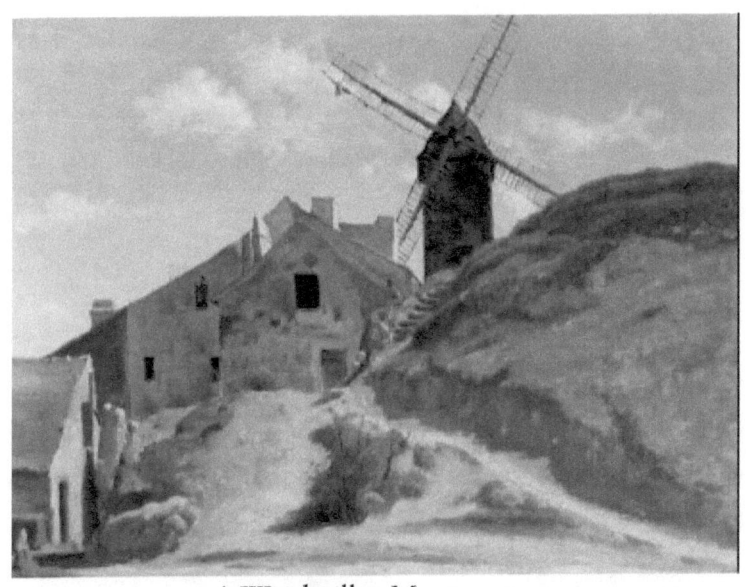

A Windmill at Montmartre
1845, oil on canvas

Maria Tsaneva

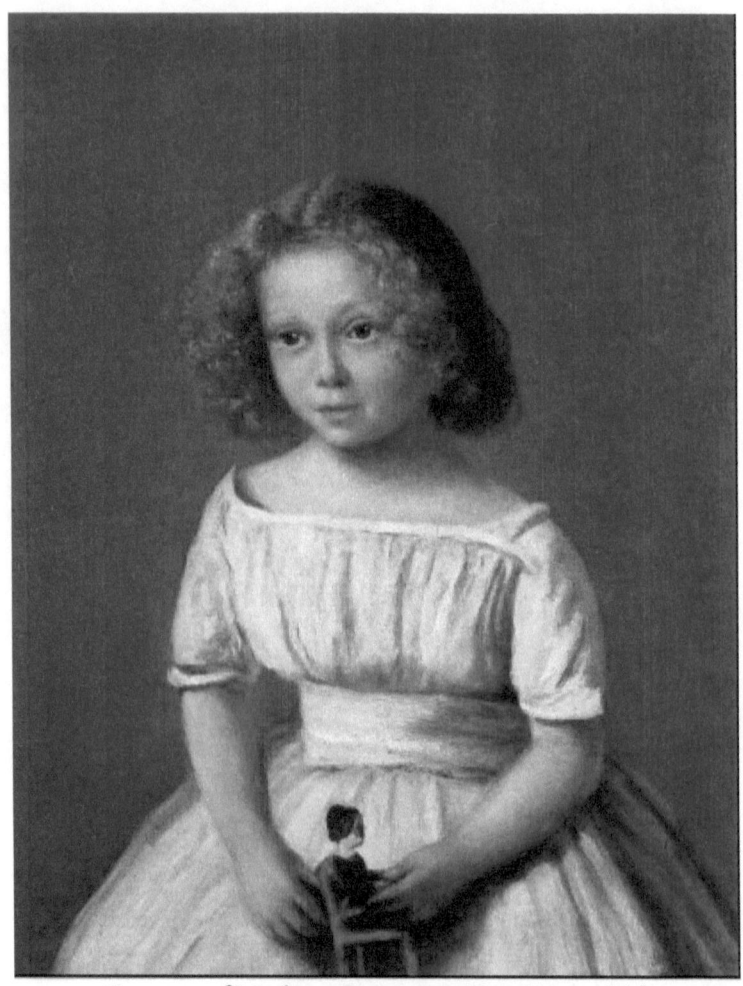

Portrait of Madame Langeron, Four Years Old
1845, oil on canvas

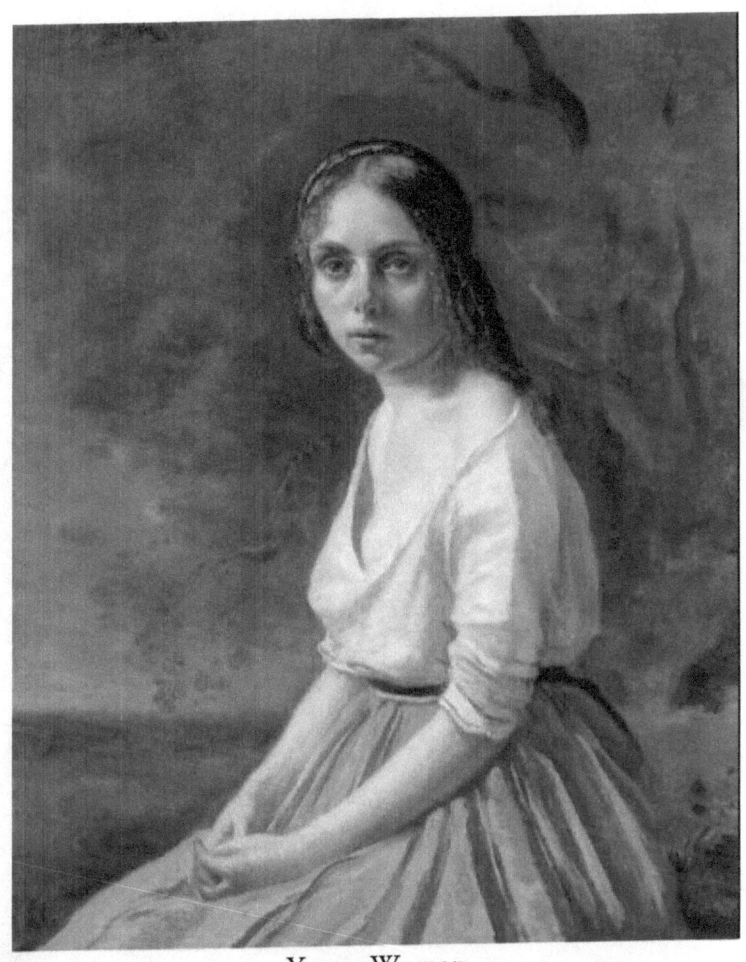

Young Woman
1845, oil on canvas

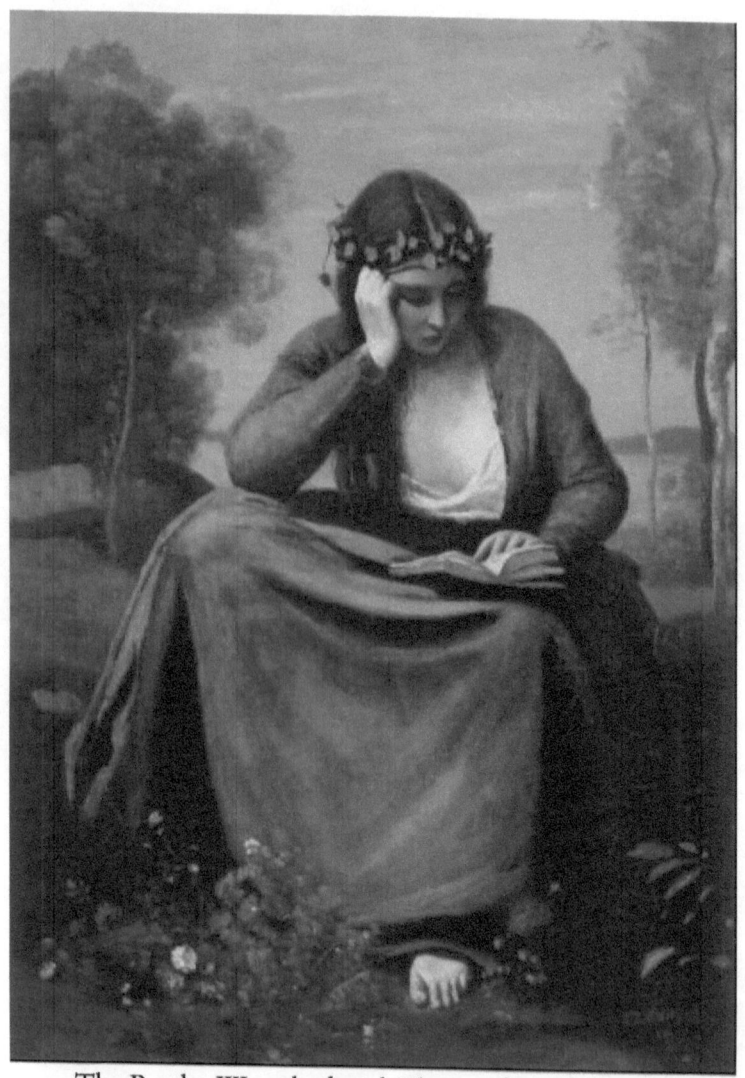

The Reader Wreathed with Flowers (Virgil's Muse)
1845, oil on canvas,

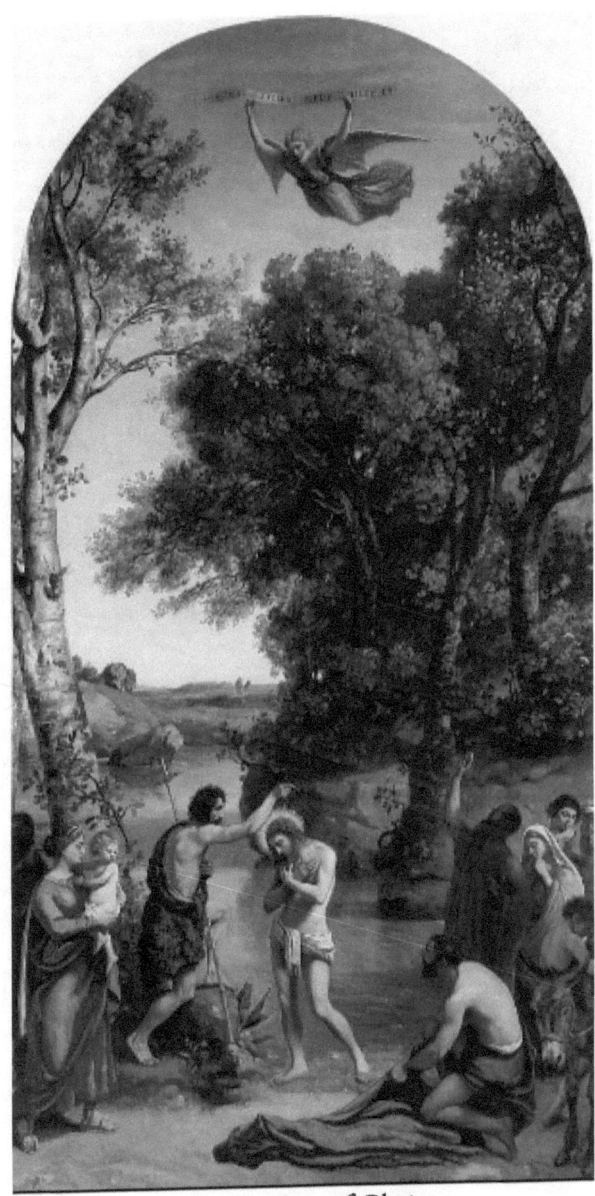

The Baptism of Christ
1845-47, oil on canvas

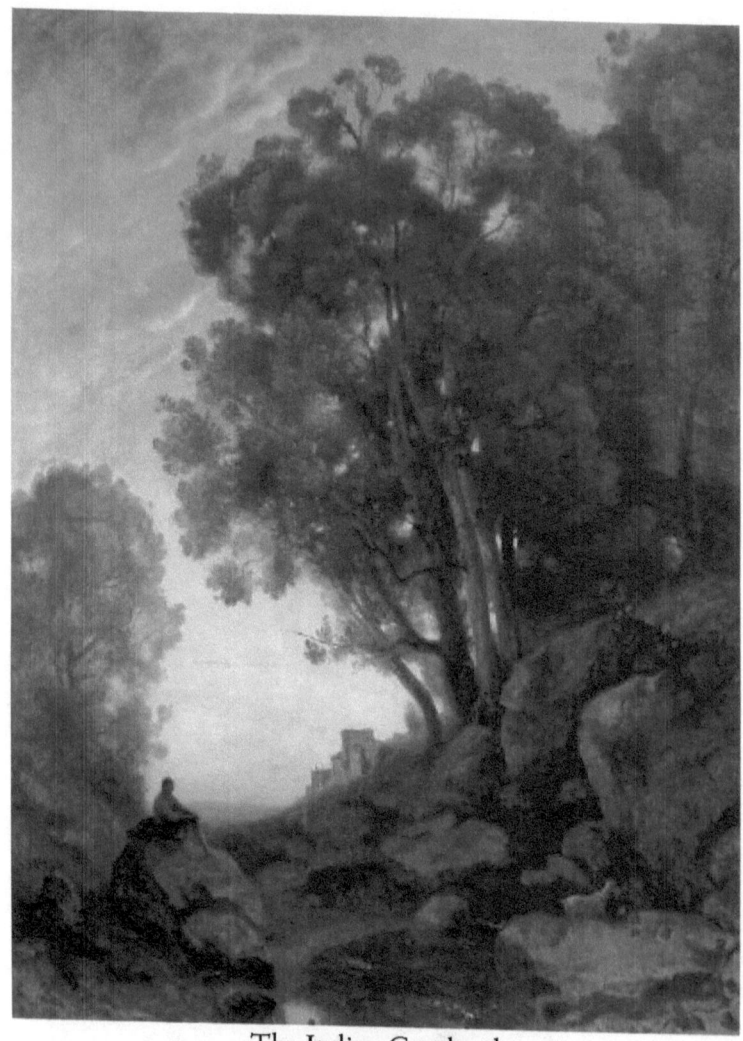

The Italian Goatherd
1847, oil on canvas

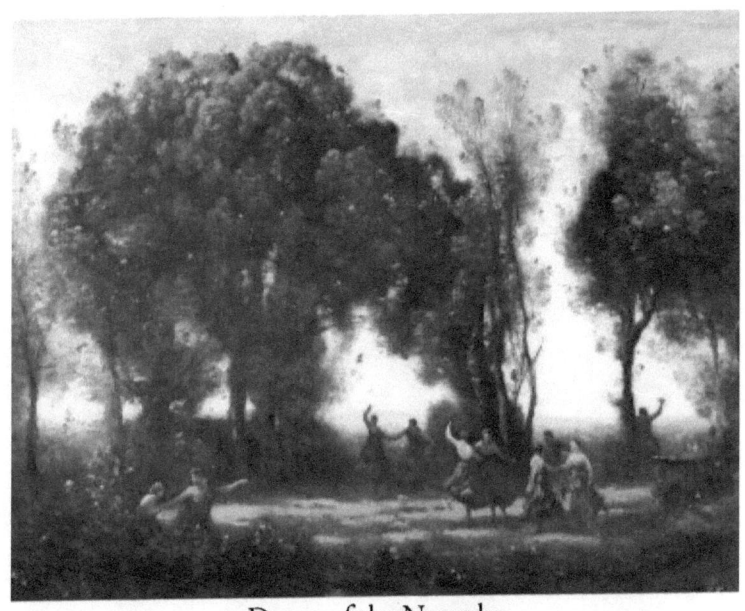

Dance of the Nymphs
1850, oil on canvas

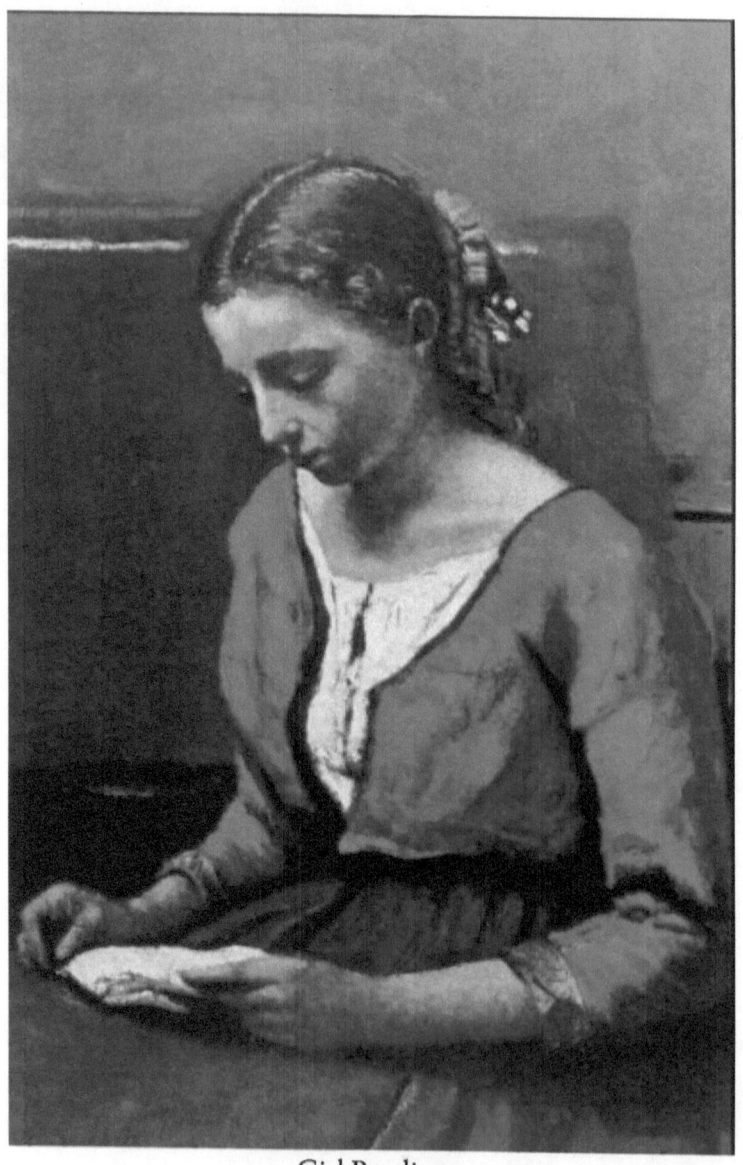

Girl Reading
1850, oil on canvas

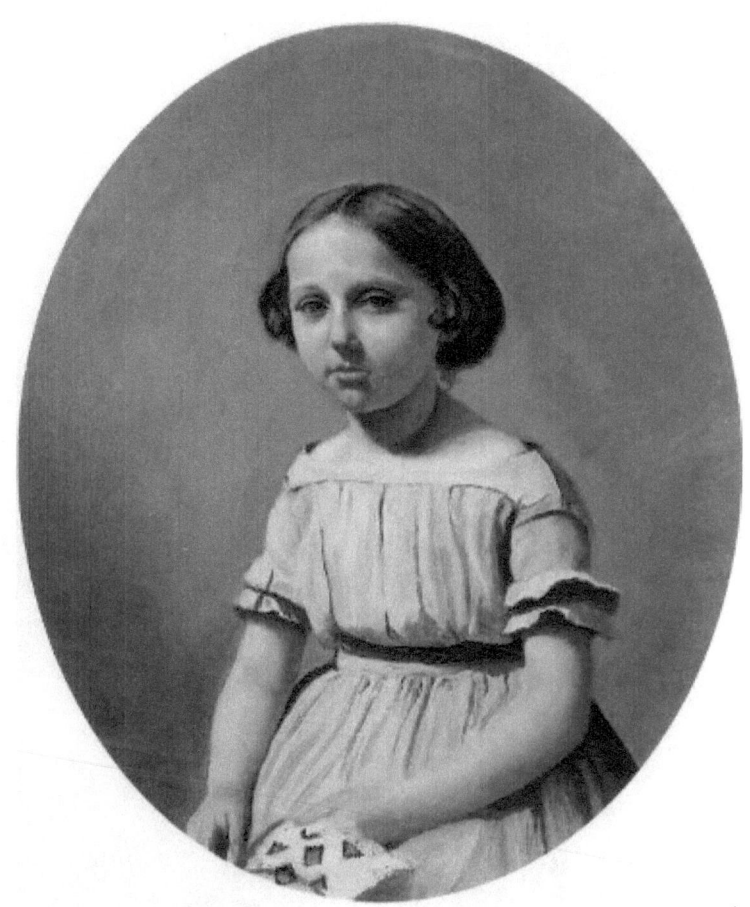

The Eldest Daughter of M. Edouard Delalain (Mme. de Graet)
1850, oil on canvas

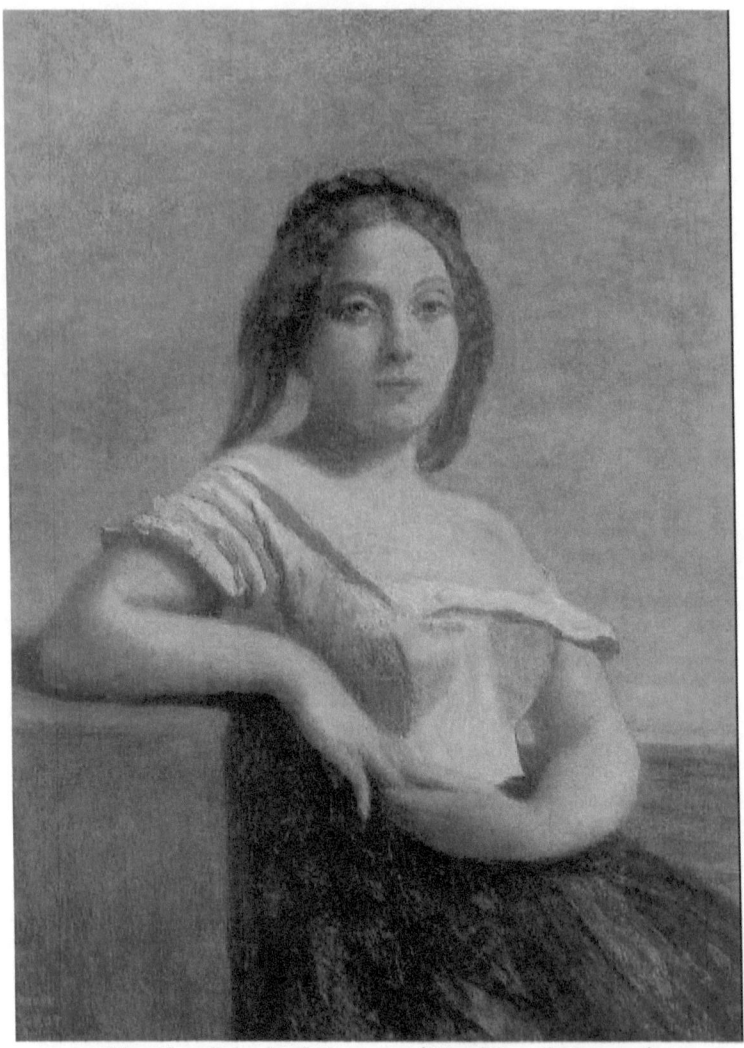

The Fair Maid of Gascony (The Blond Gascon)
1850, oil on canvas

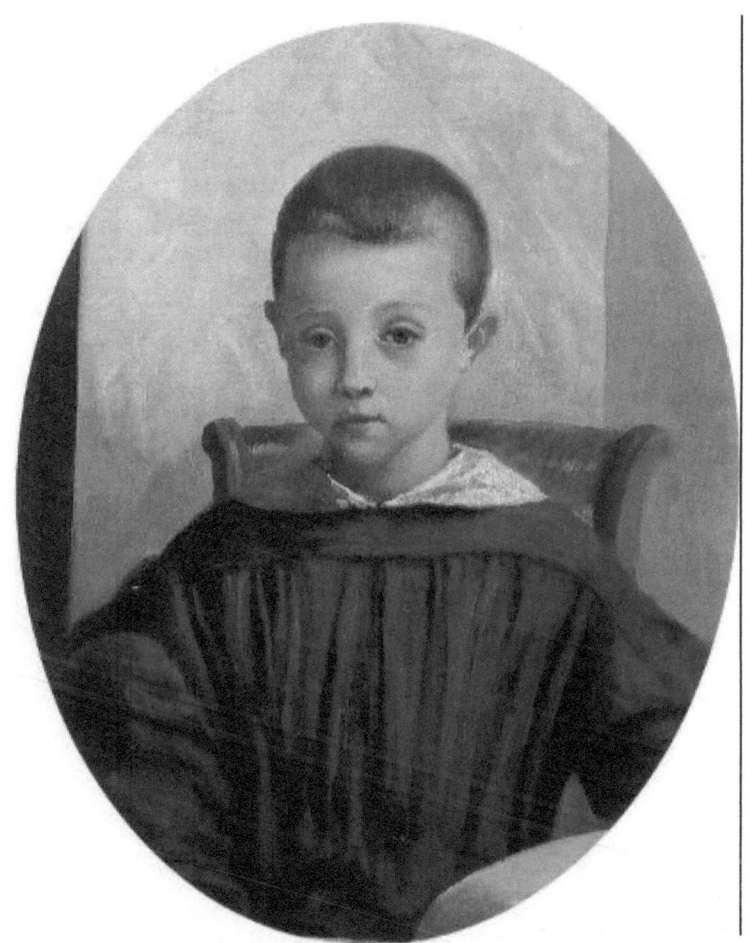

The Son of M. Edouard Delalain
1850, oil on canvas

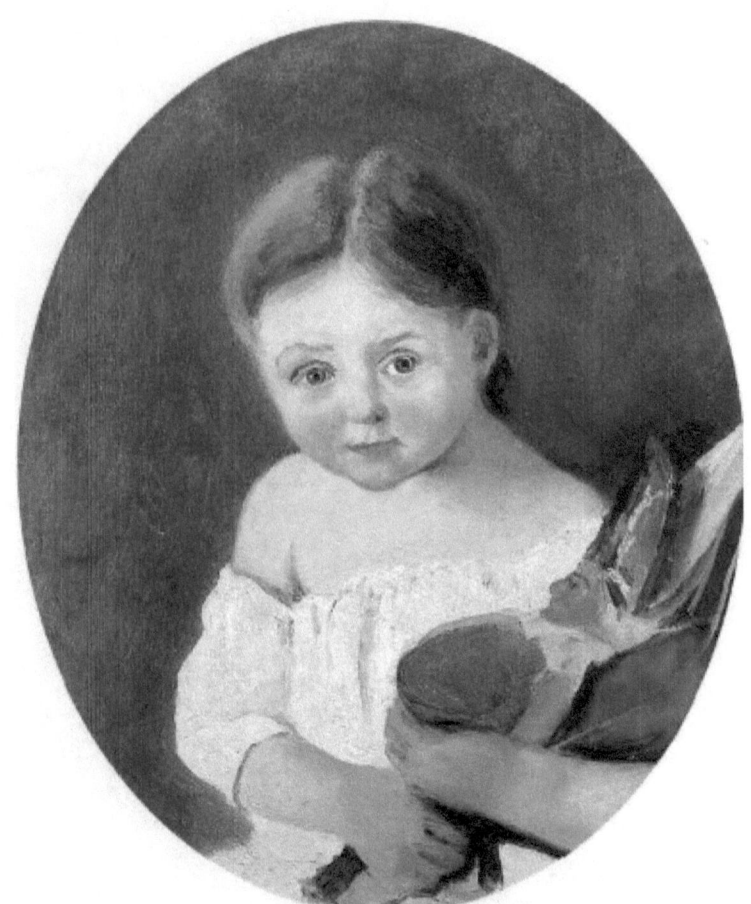

The Youngest Daughter of M. Edouard Delalain
1850, oil on canvas

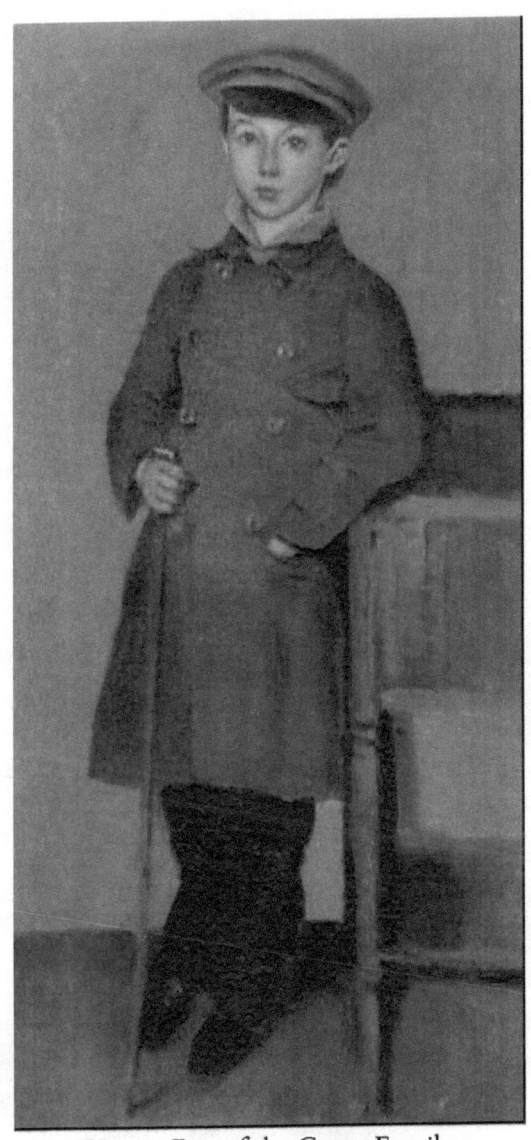

Young Boy of the Corot Family
1850, oil on canvas

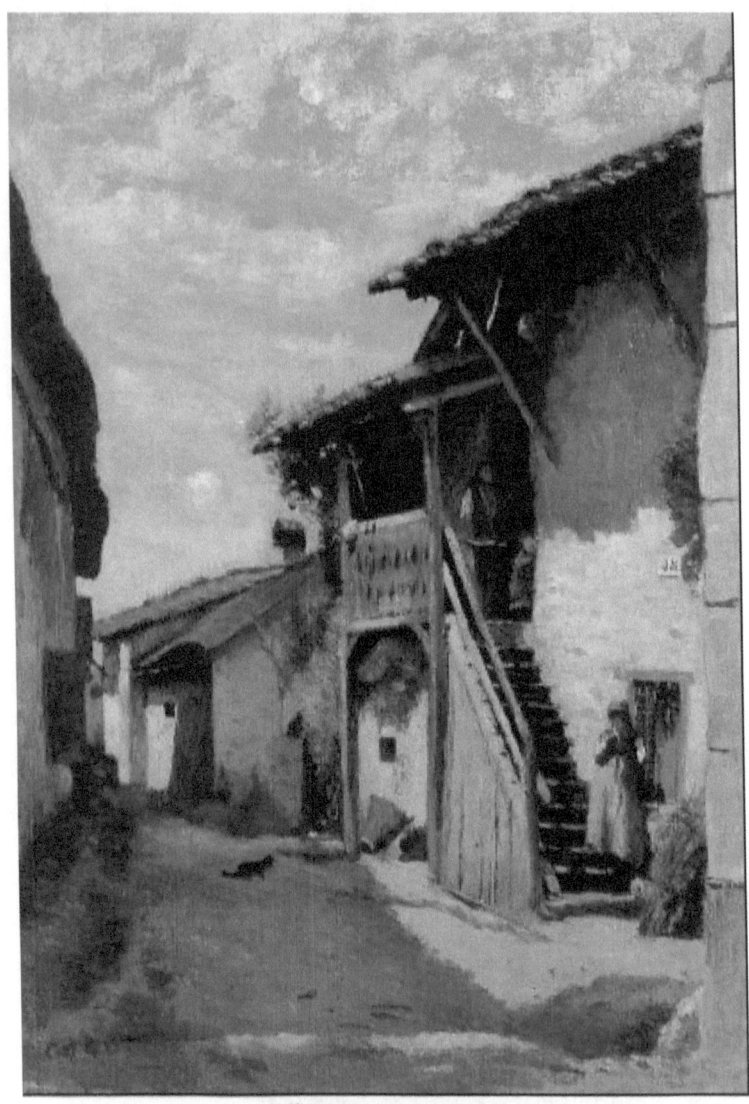

A Village Street, Dardagny
1853, oil on canvas

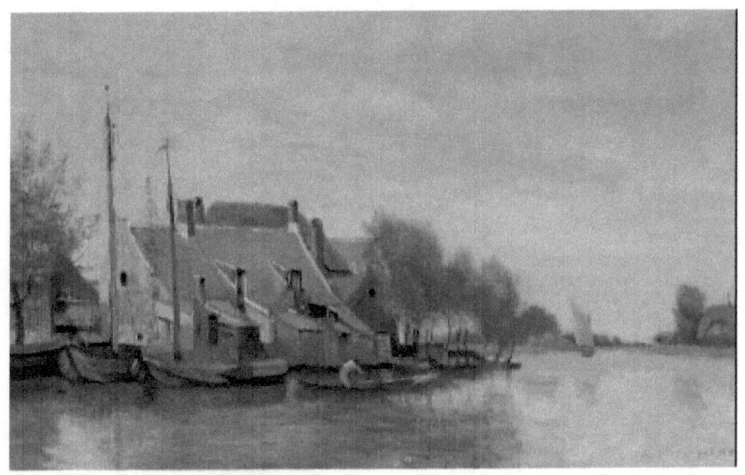

Near Rotterdam, Small Houses on the Banks of a Canal
1854, oil on canvas

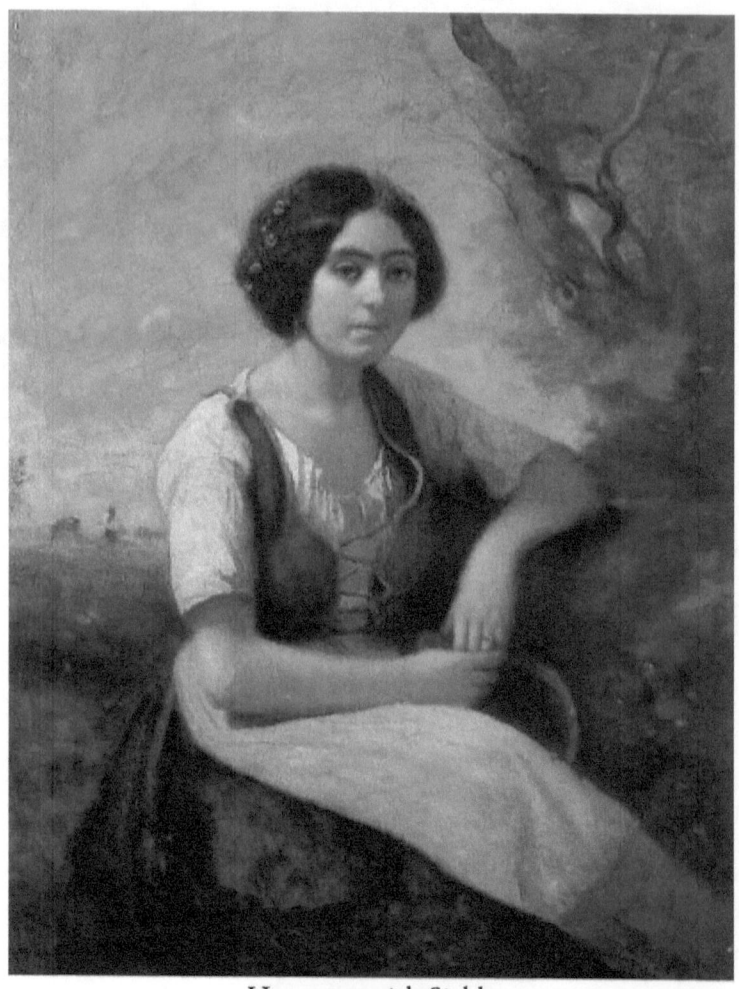

Harvester with Sickle
1855, oil on canvas

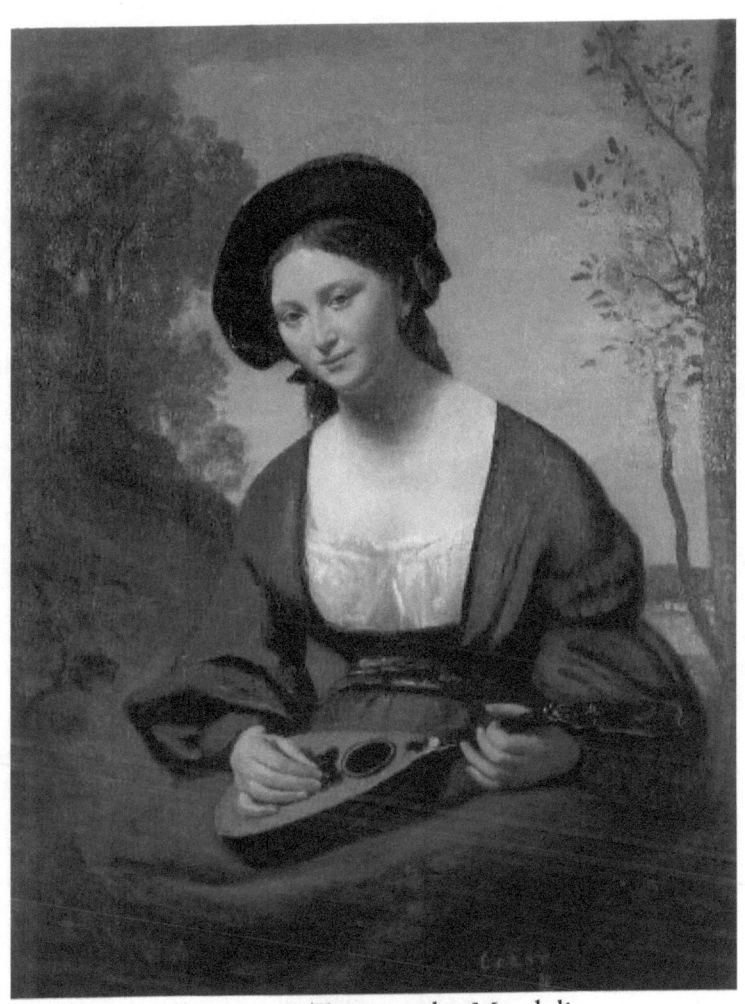

Woman in a Toque with a Mandolin
1855, oil on canvas

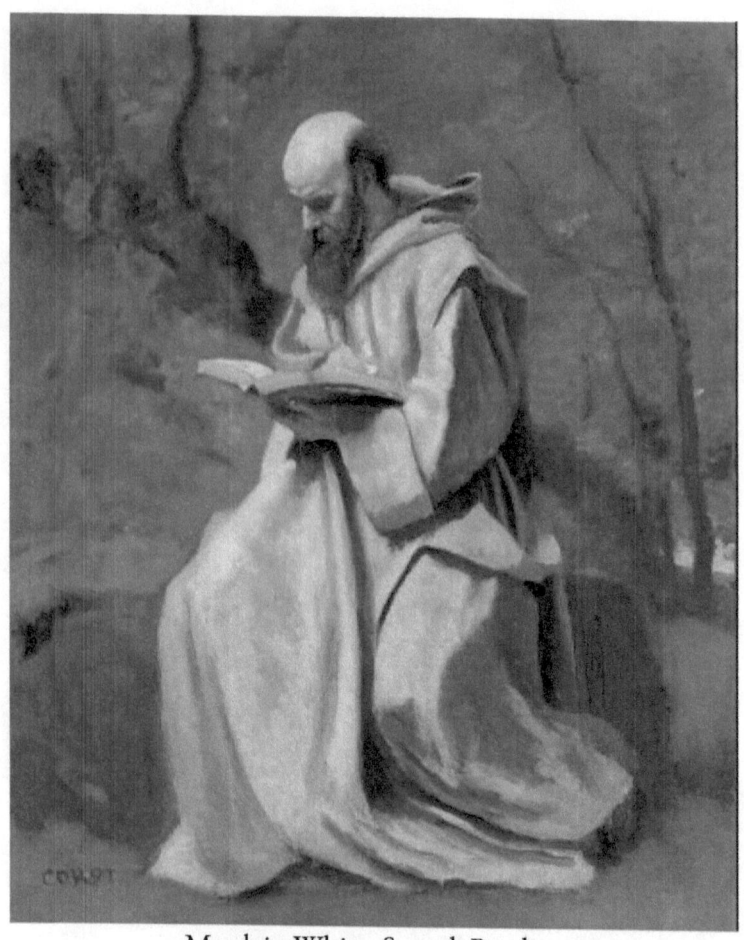

Monk in White, Seated, Reading
1857, oil on canvas

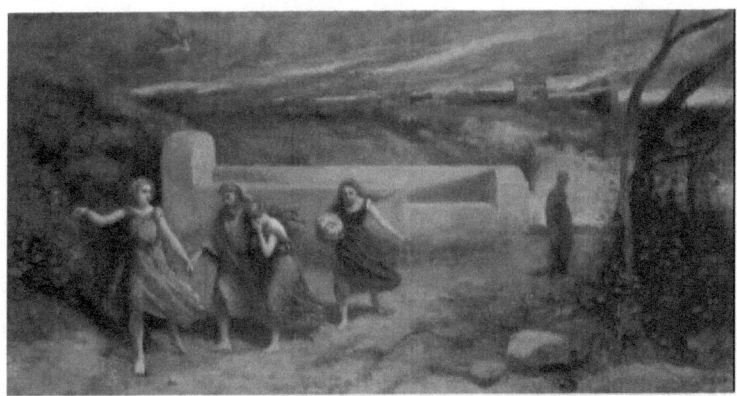

The Destruction of Sodom
1857, oil on canvas

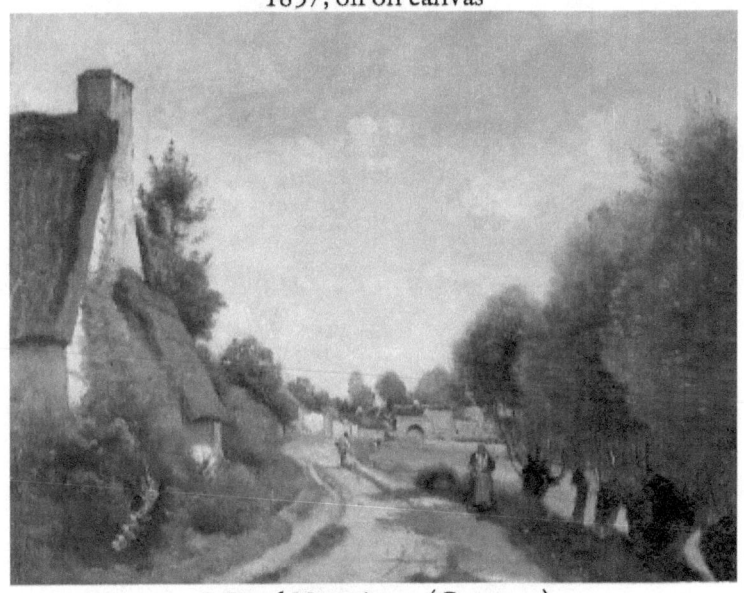

A Road Near Arras (Cottages)
1858, oil on canvas

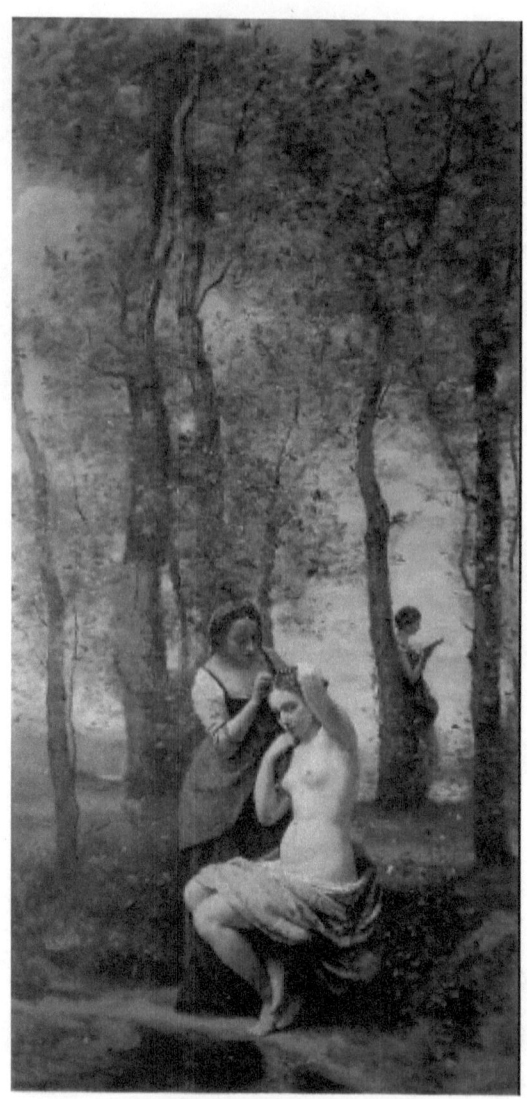

Landscape with Figures
1859, oil on canvas

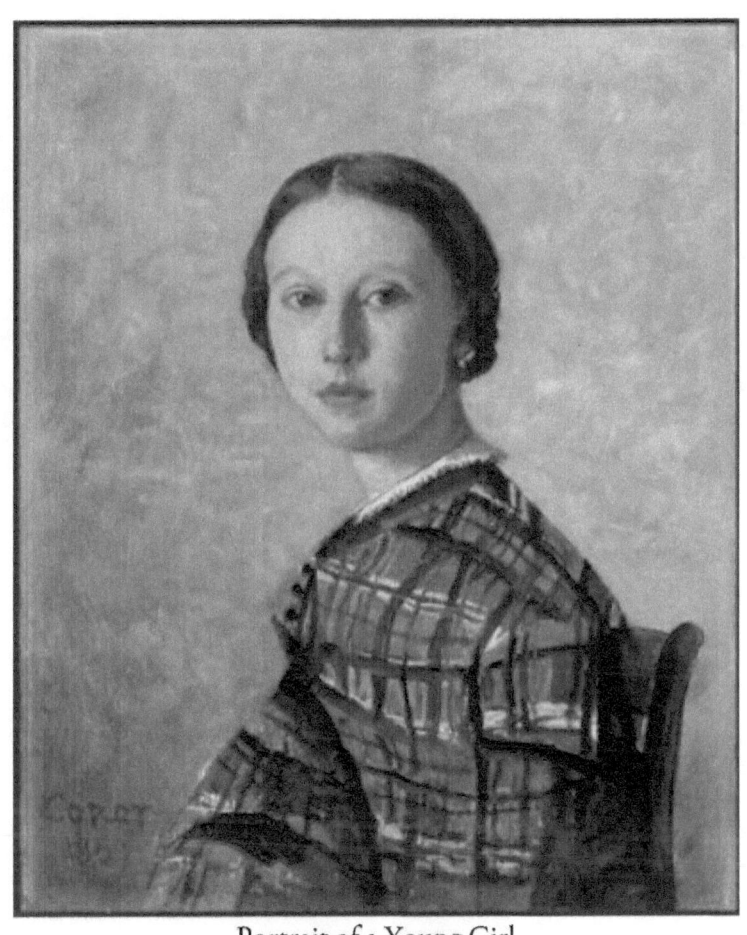

Portrait of a Young Girl
1859, oil on canvas

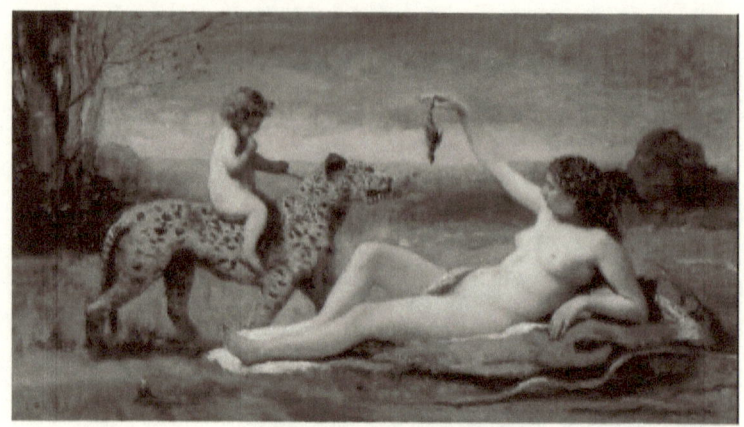

Bacchante with a Panther
1860, oil on canvas

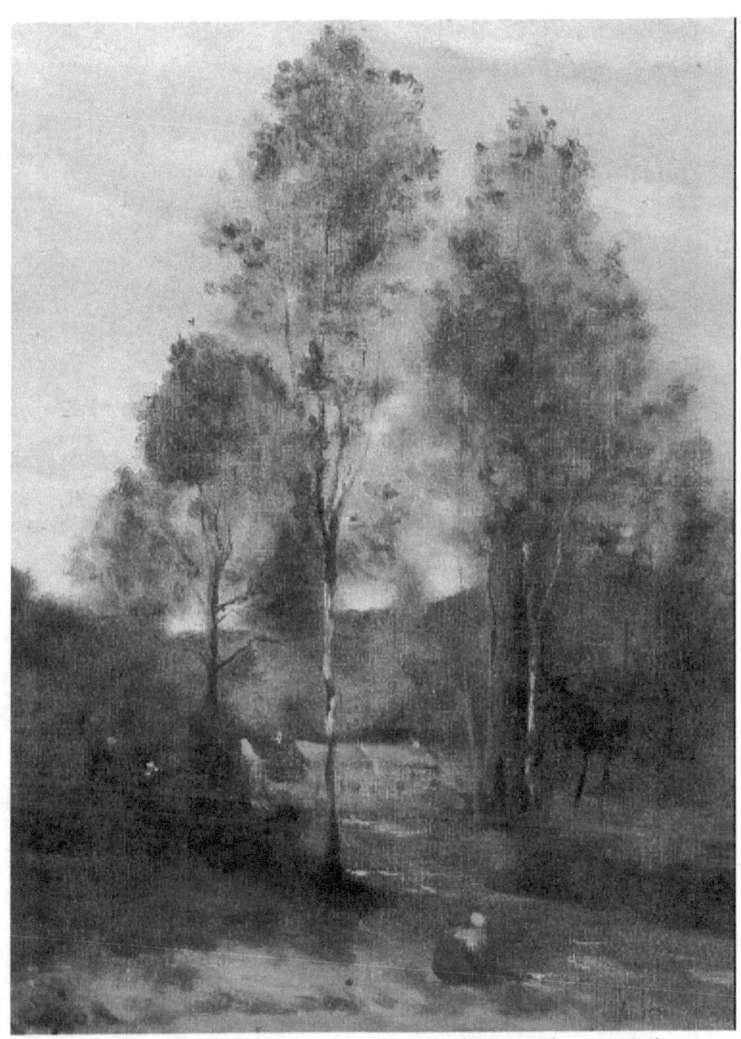

Clearing in the Bois Pierre, at Eveaux near Chateau Thiery
1860, oil on canvas

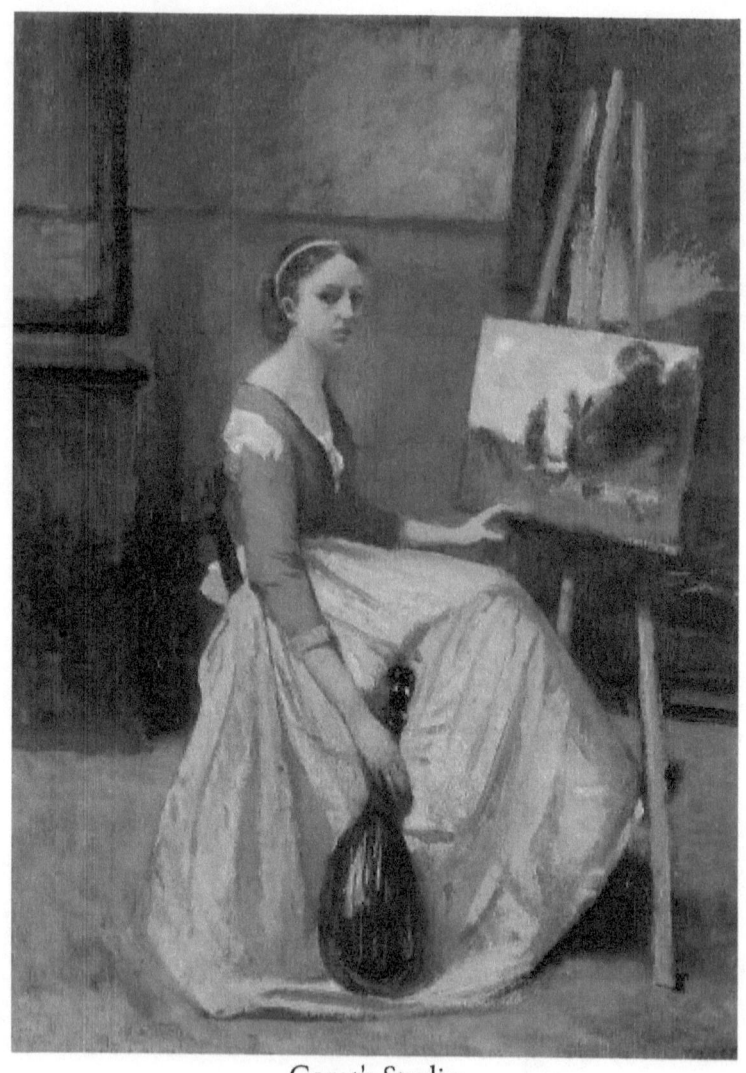

Corot's Studio
1860, oil on canvas

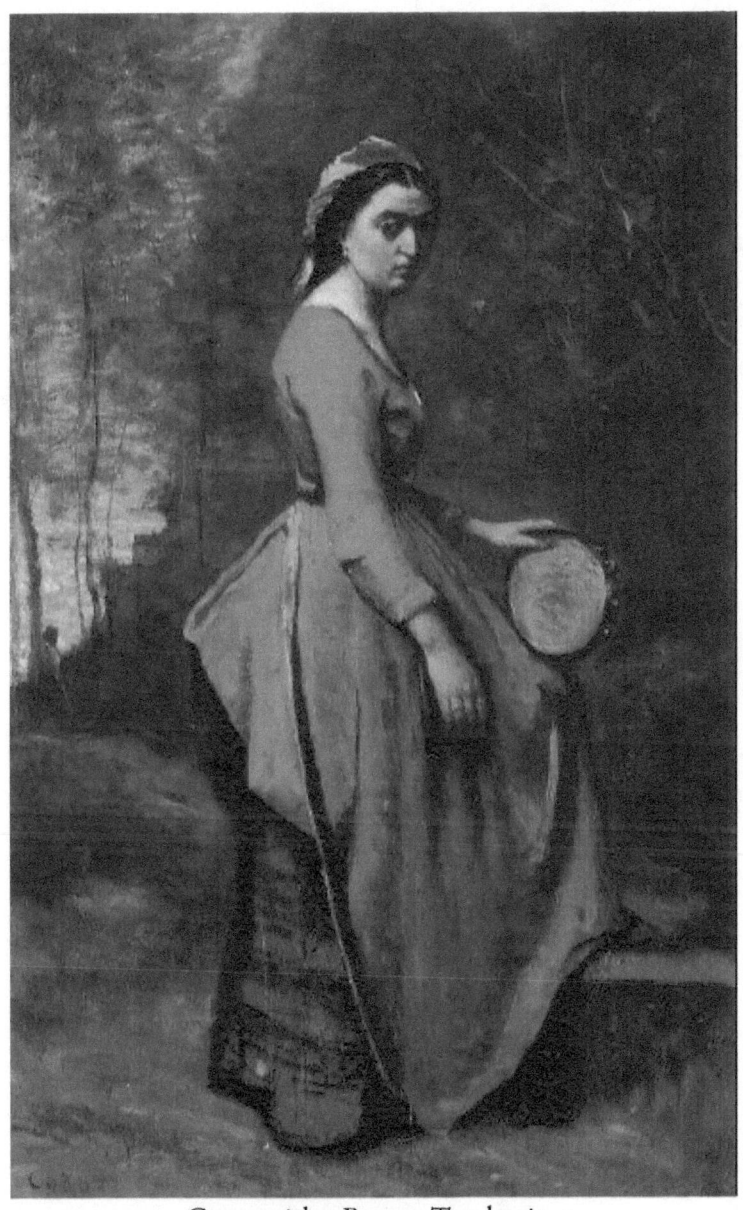

Gypsy with a Basque Tamborine
1860, oil on canvas

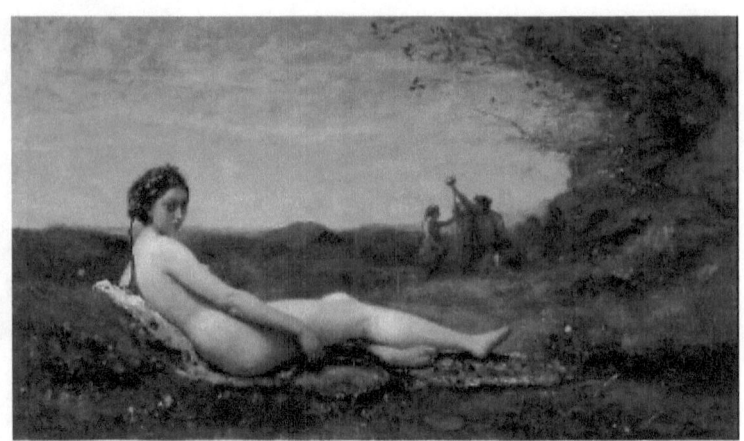

Repose
1860, oil on canvas

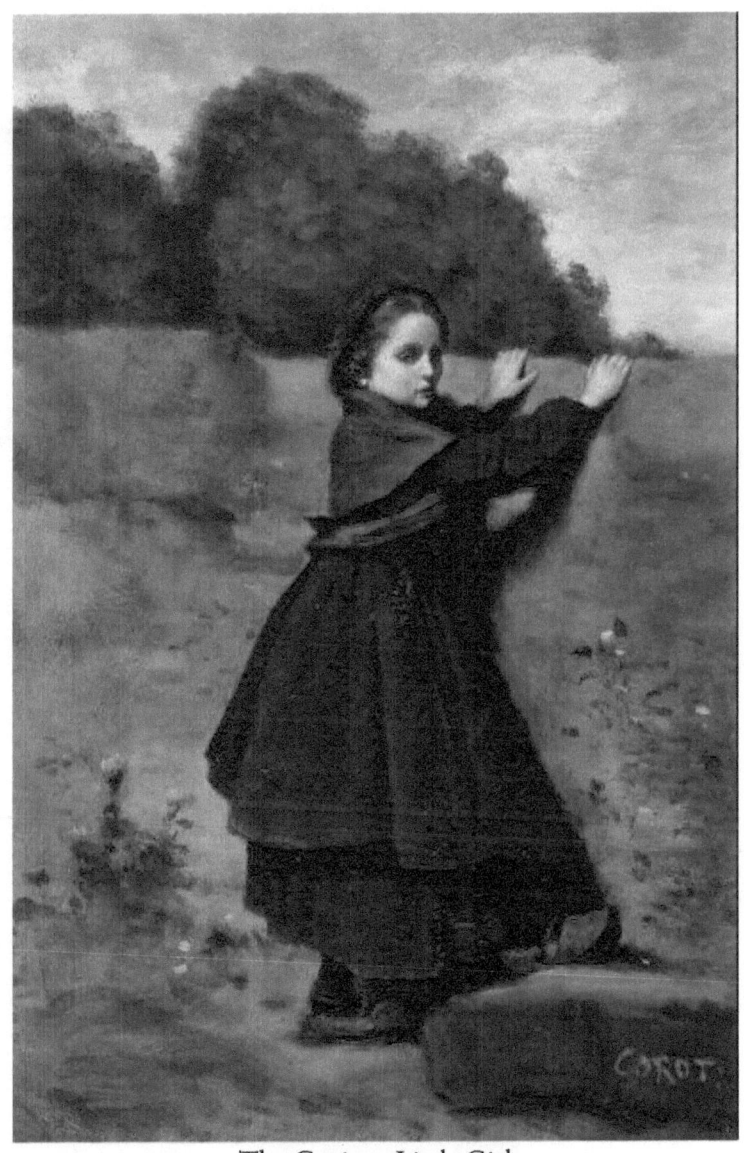

The Curious Little Girl
1860, oil on canvas

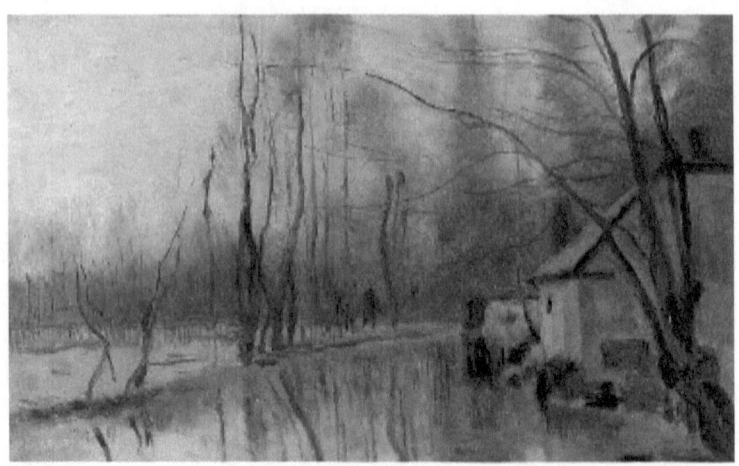

Voisinlieu, House by the Water
1860, oil on canvas

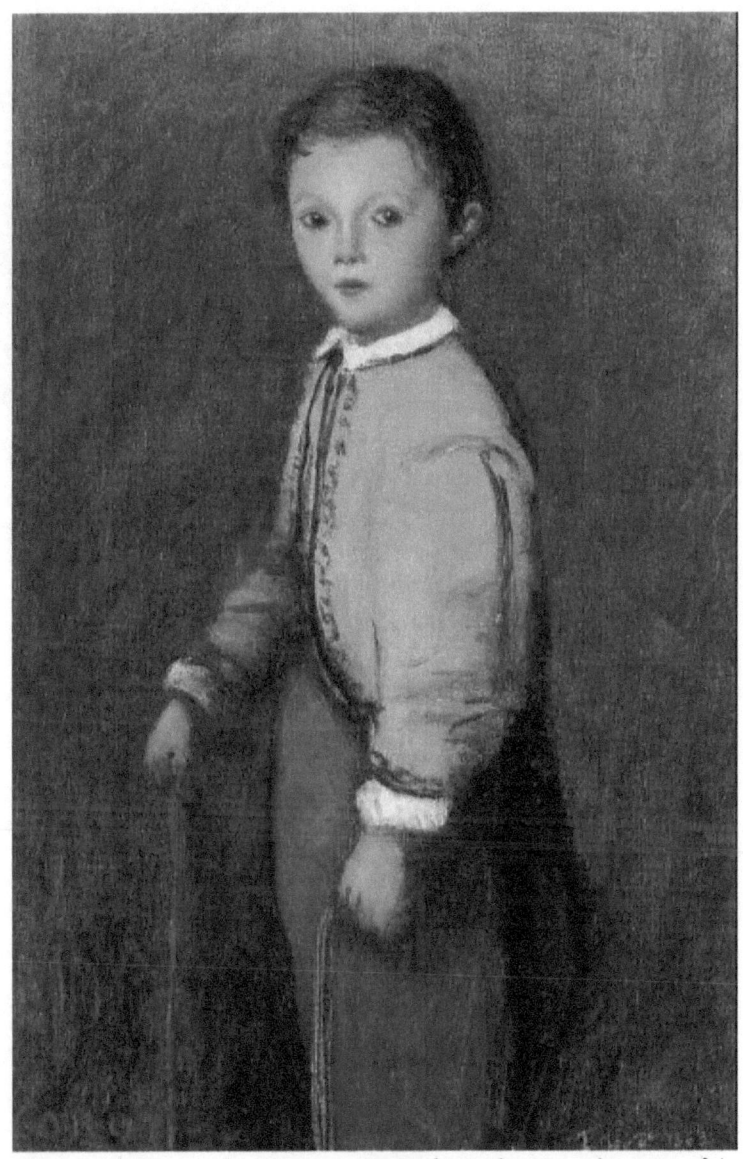

Fernand Corot, the Painter s Grand Nephew, at the Age of 4
and a Half Years
1863, oil on canvas

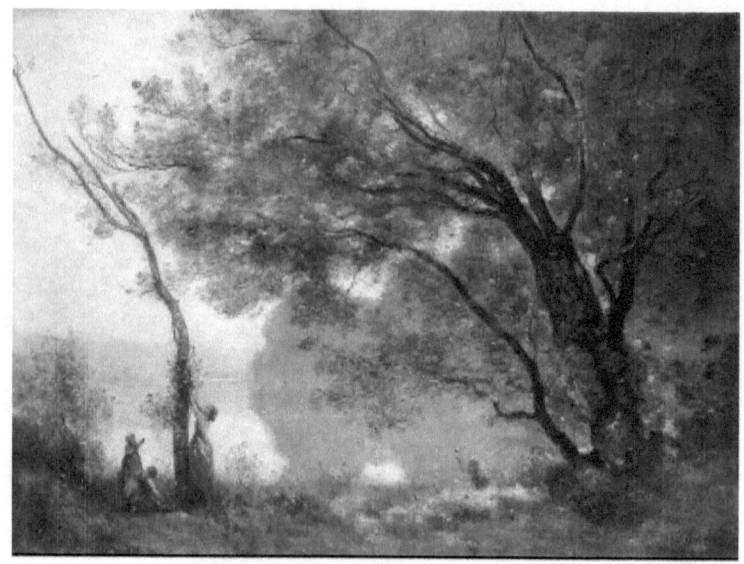

Recollections of Mortefontaine
1864, oil on canvas

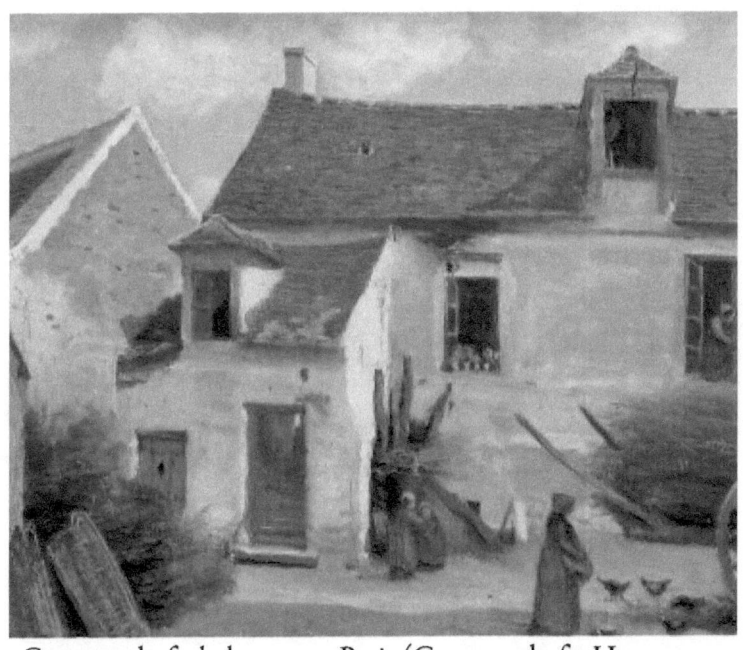

Courtyard of a bakery near Paris (Courtyard of a House near Paris)
1865, oil on canvas

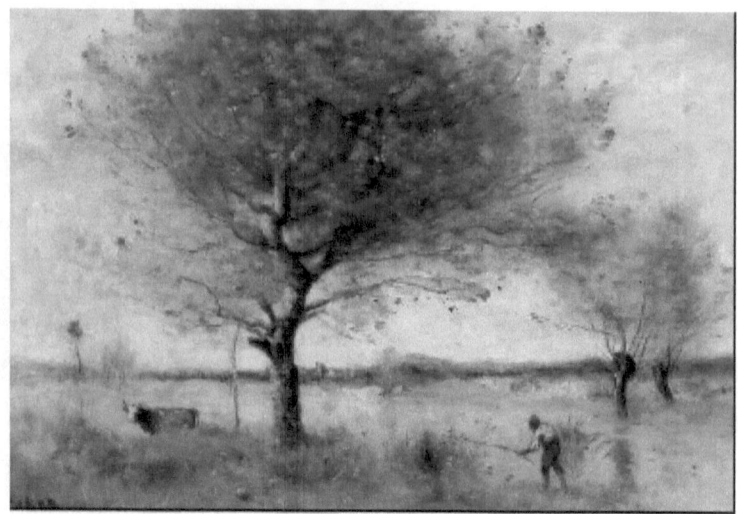

Pond with a Large Tree
1865, oil on canvas

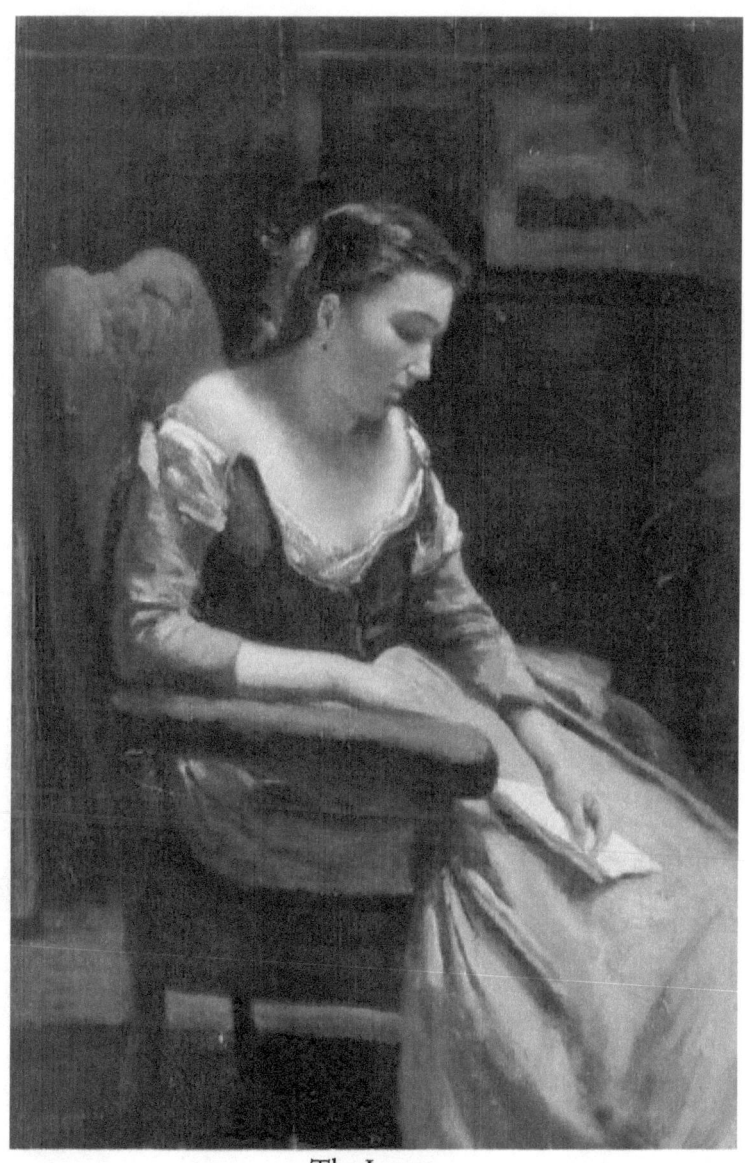

The Letter
1865, oil on canvas

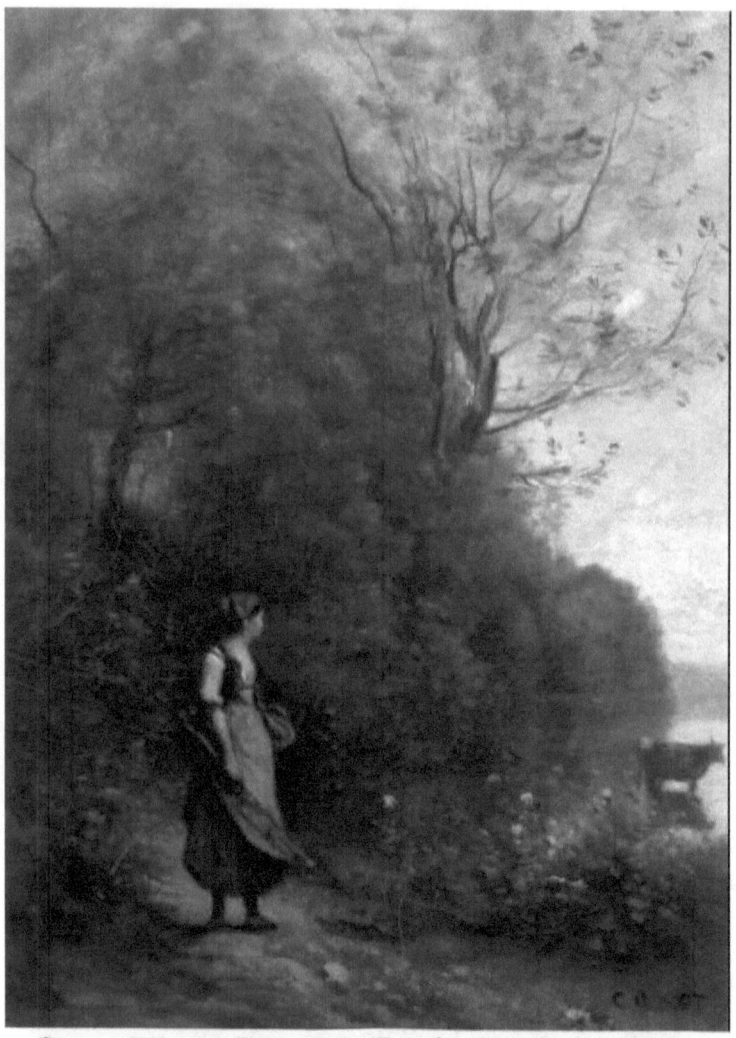

Peasant Woman Pasturing a Cow by the Edge of a Forest
1865-70, oil on canvas

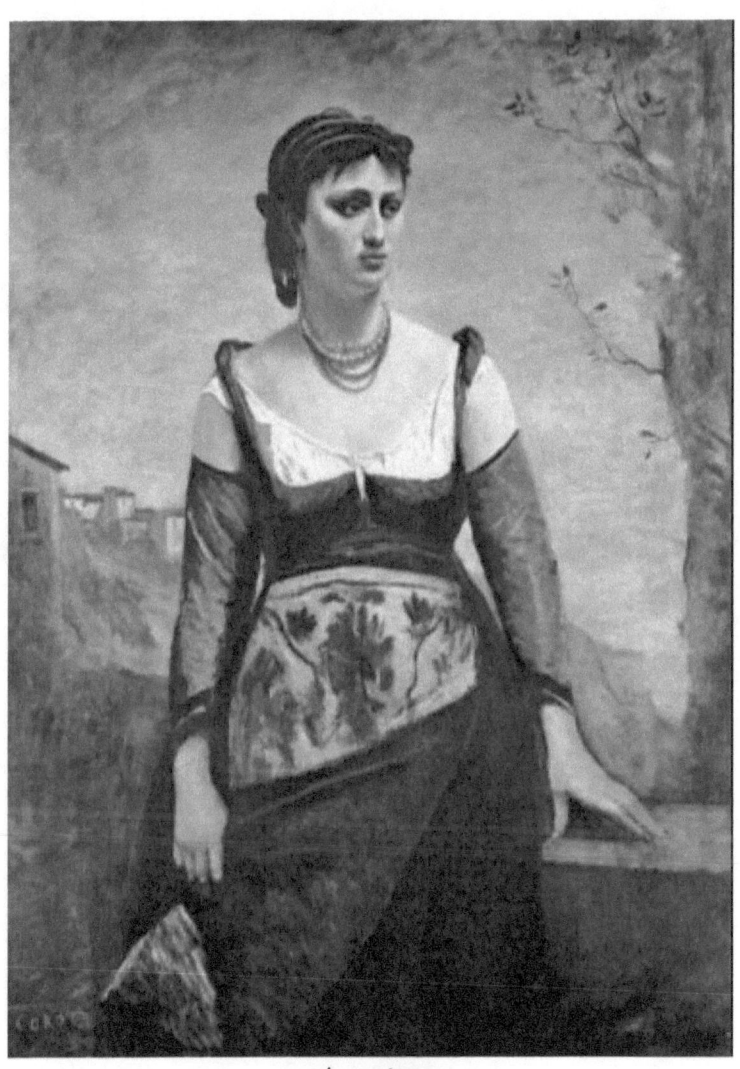

Agostina
1866, oil on canvas

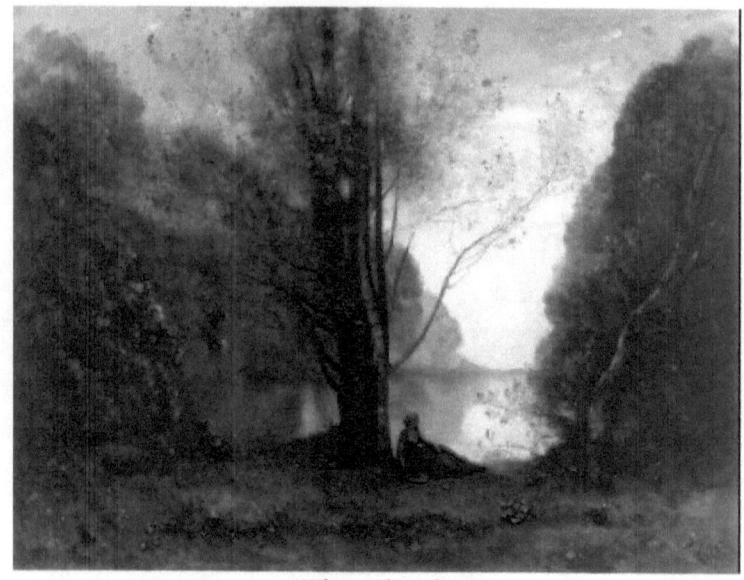

The Solitude
1866, oil on canvas

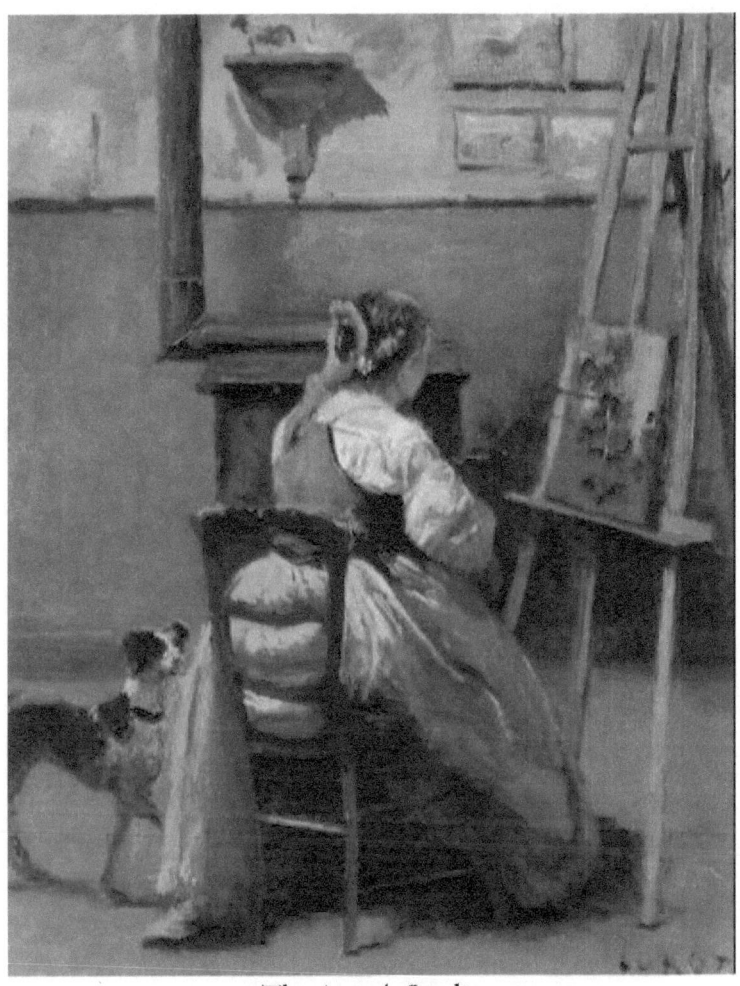

The Artist's Studio
1868, oil on canvas

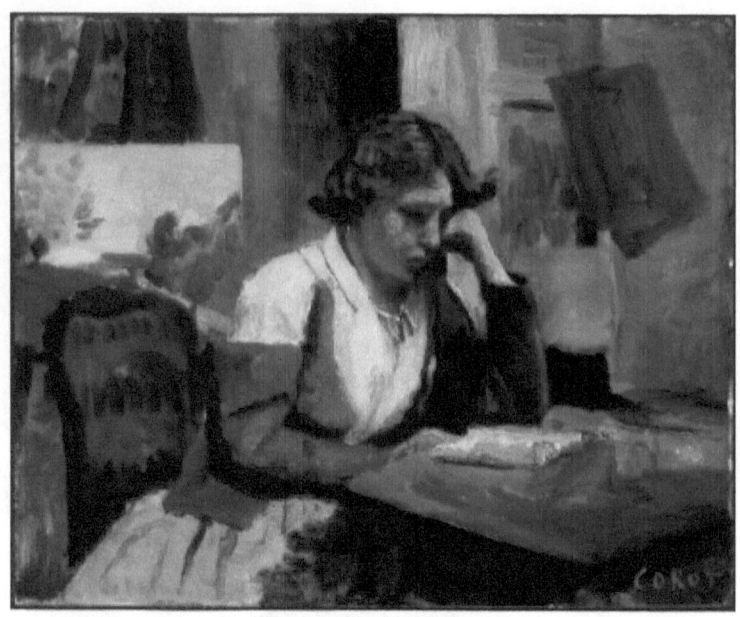

Young Girl Reading
1868, oil on canvas

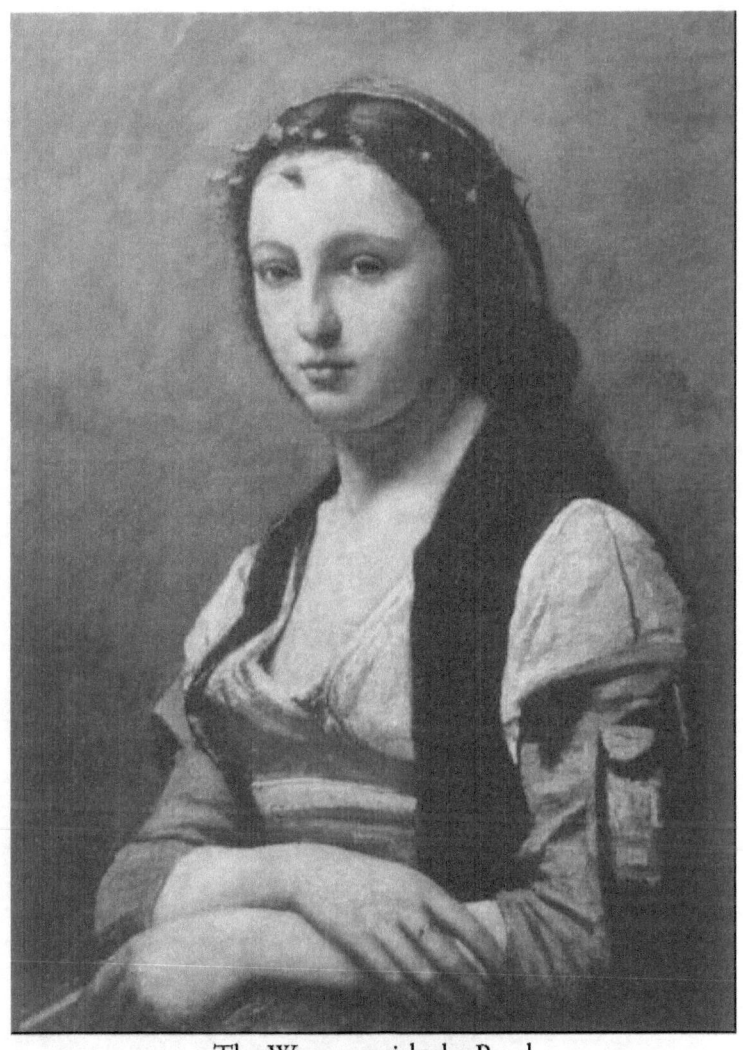

The Woman with the Pearl
1868-70, oil on canvas

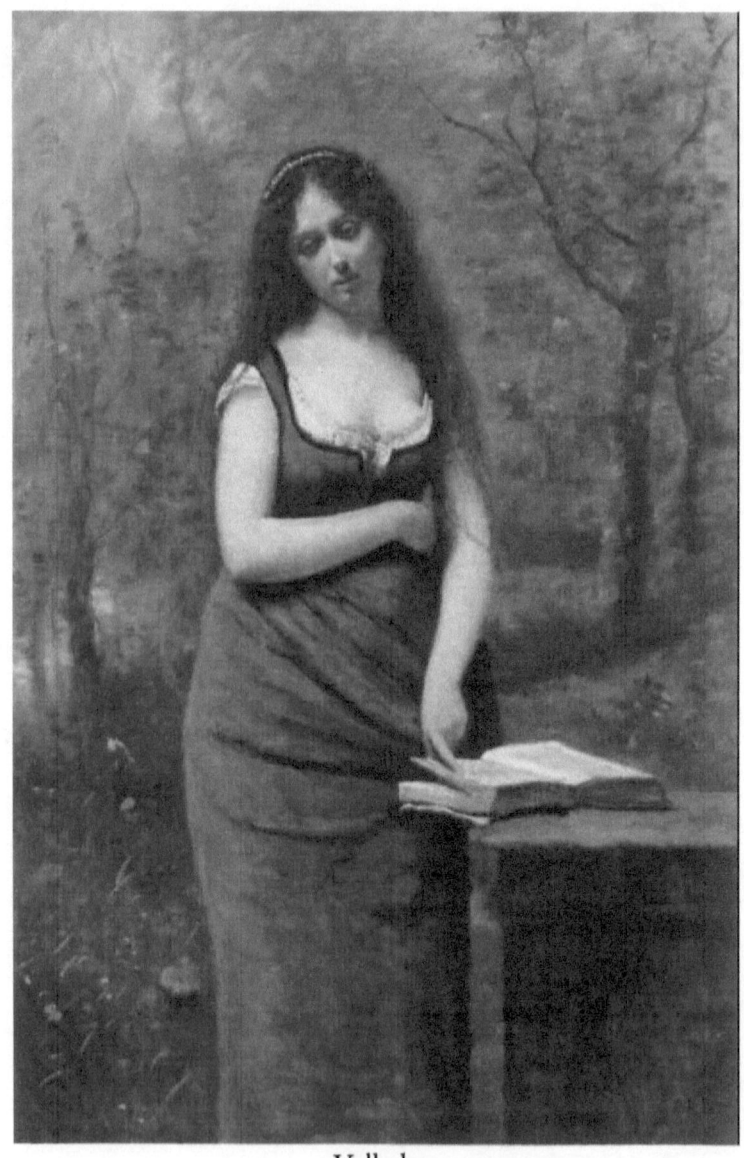

Valleda
1868-70, oil on wood,

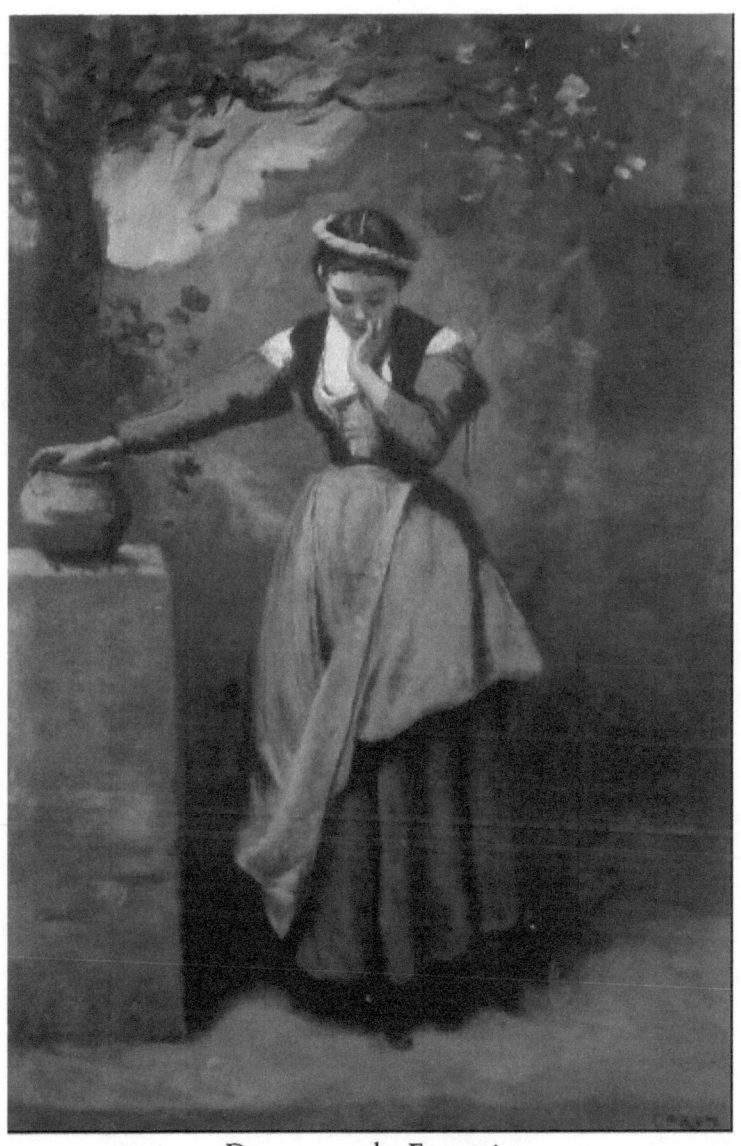

Dreamer at the Fountain
1870, oil on canvas

Maria Tsaneva

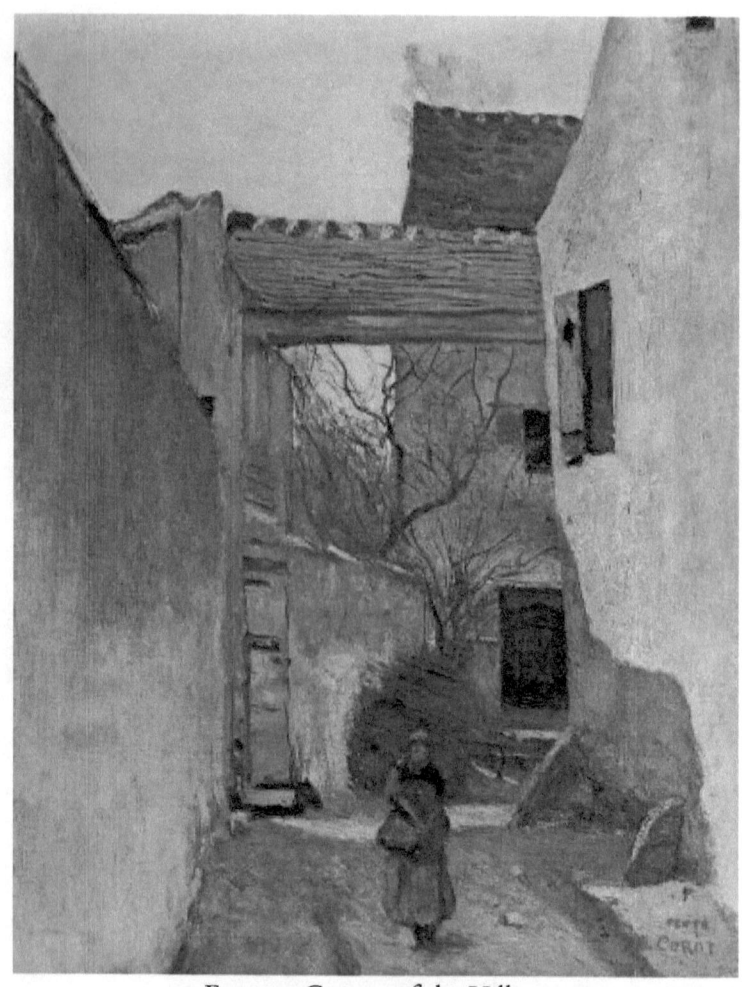

Ecouen, Corner of the Village
1870, oil on canvas

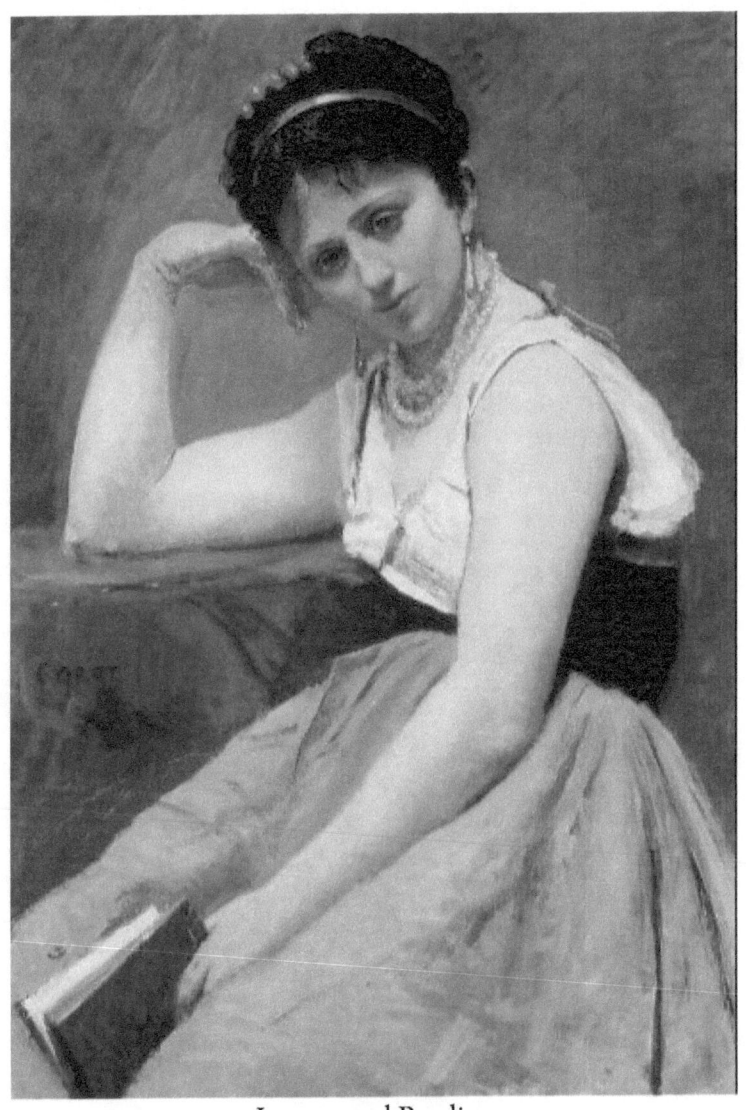

Interrupted Reading
1870, oil on canvas

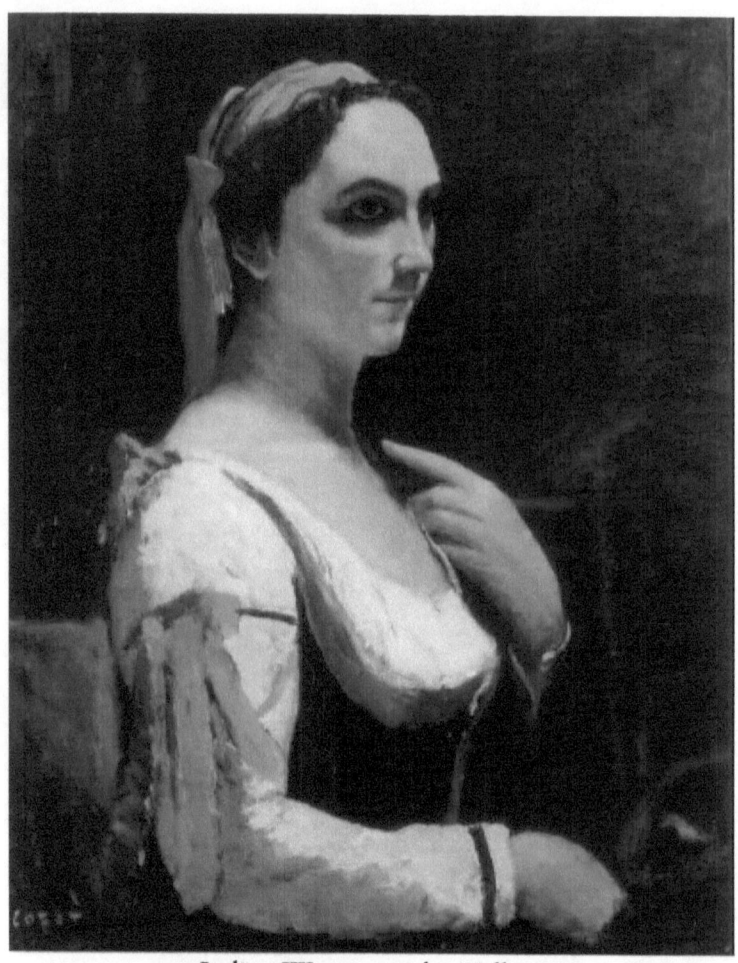

Italian Woman with a Yellow
1870, oil on canvas

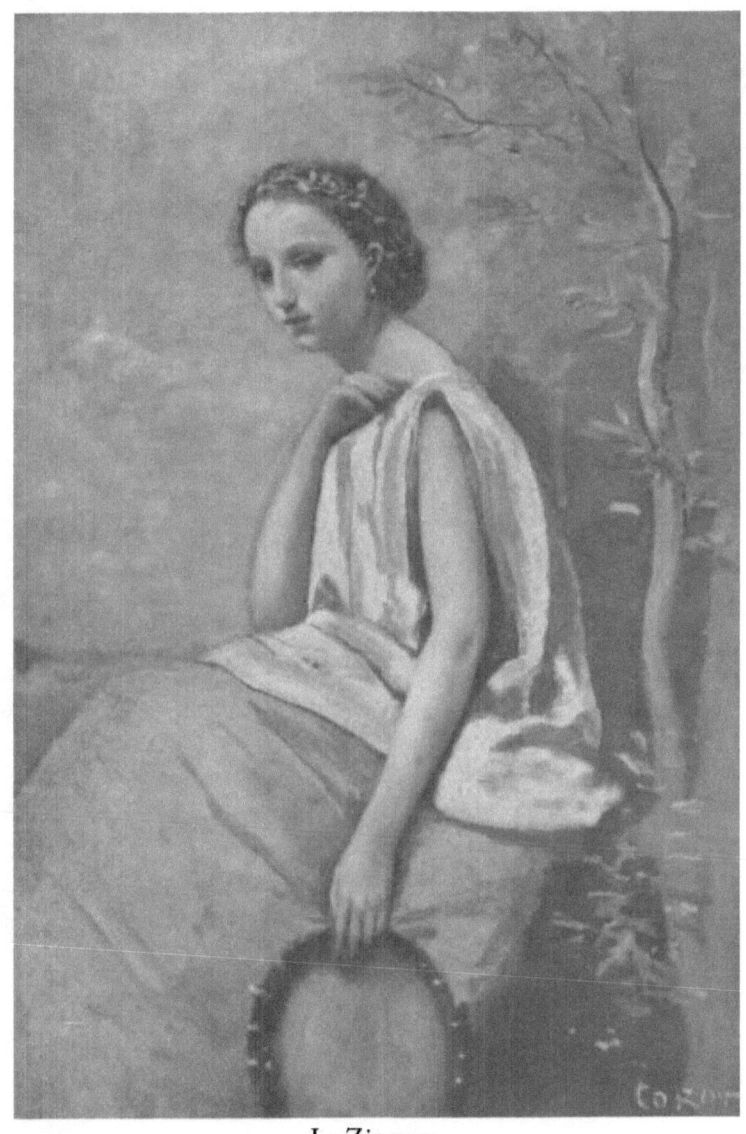

La Zingara
1870, oil on canvas

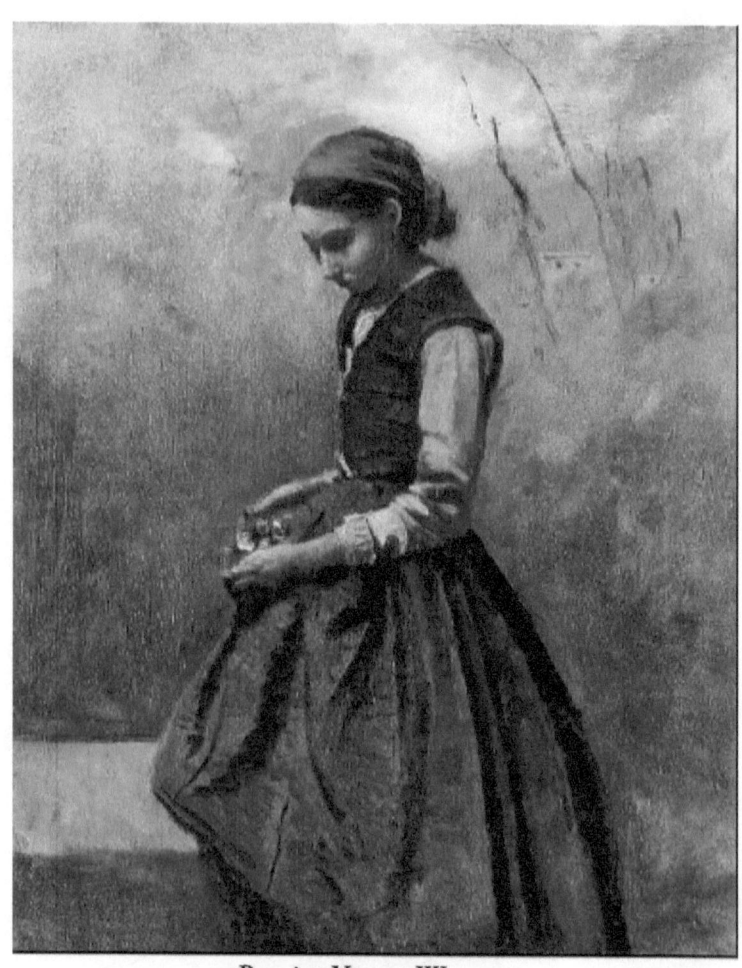

Pensive Young Woman
1870, oil on canvas

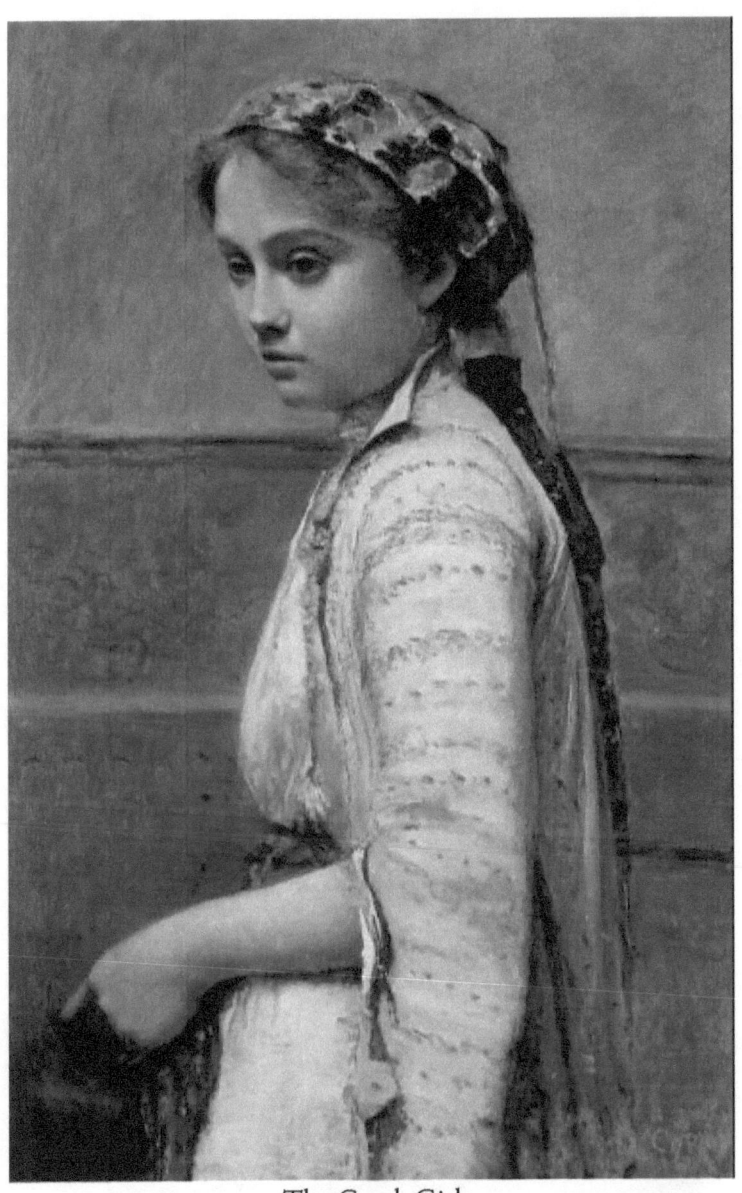

The Greek Girl
1870, oil on canvas

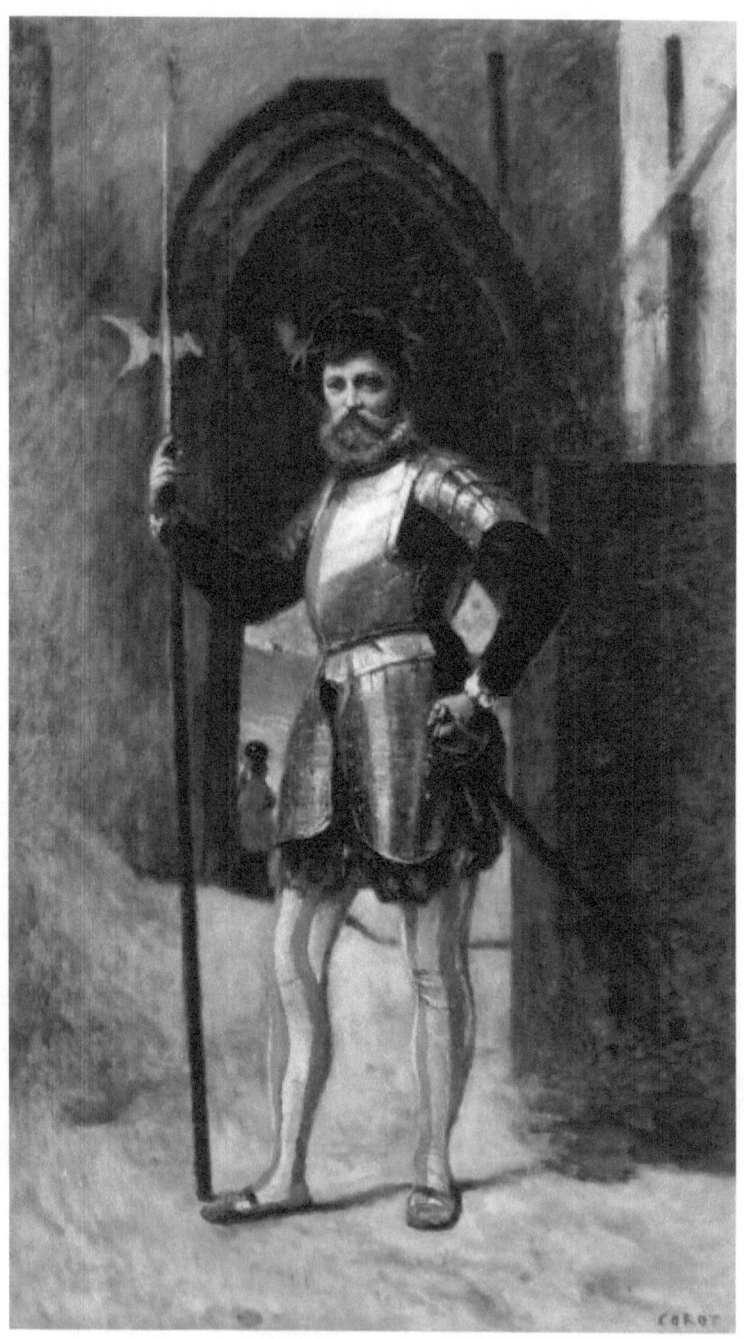

The Halberdsman
1870, oil on canvas

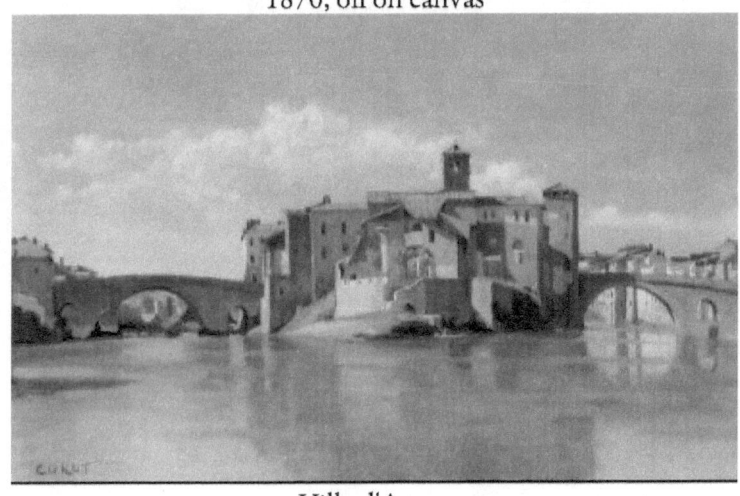

Ville d'Avray
1870, oil on canvas

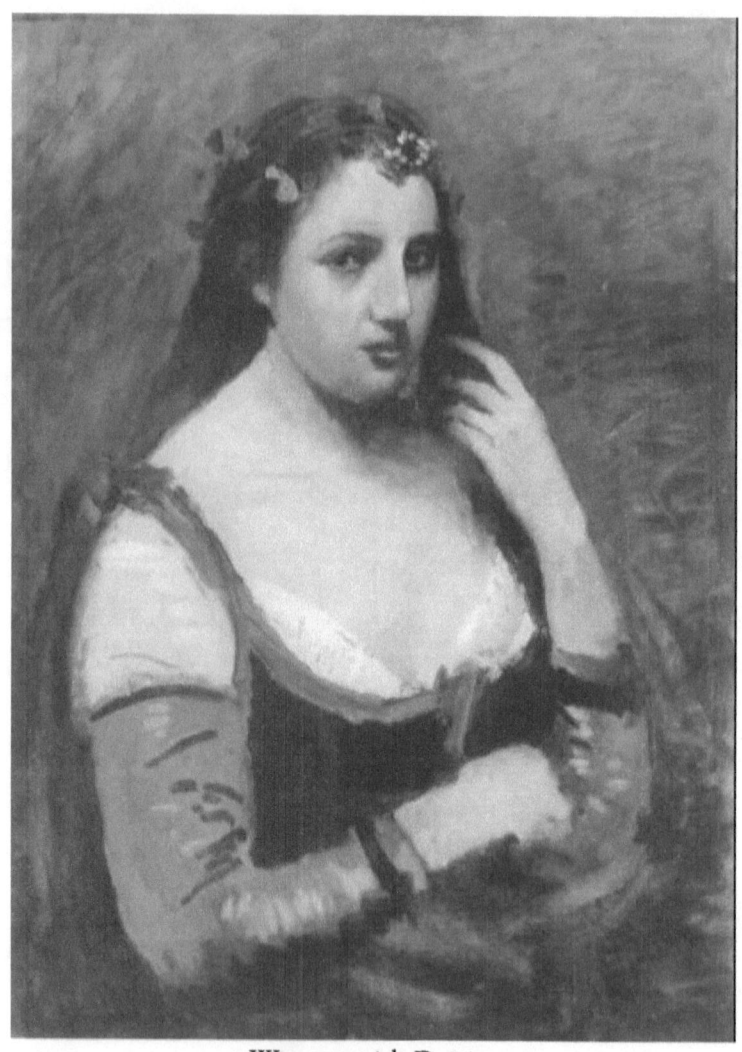

Woman with Daisies
1870, oil on canvas

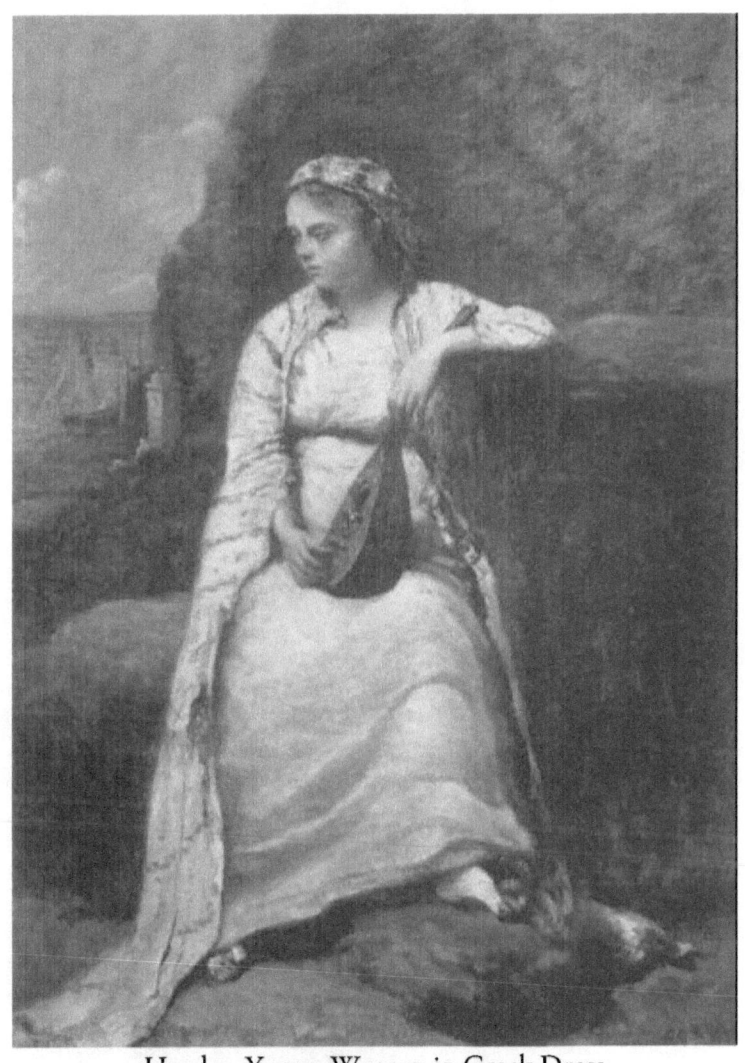

Haydee, Young Woman in Greek Dress
1870-72, oil on canvas,

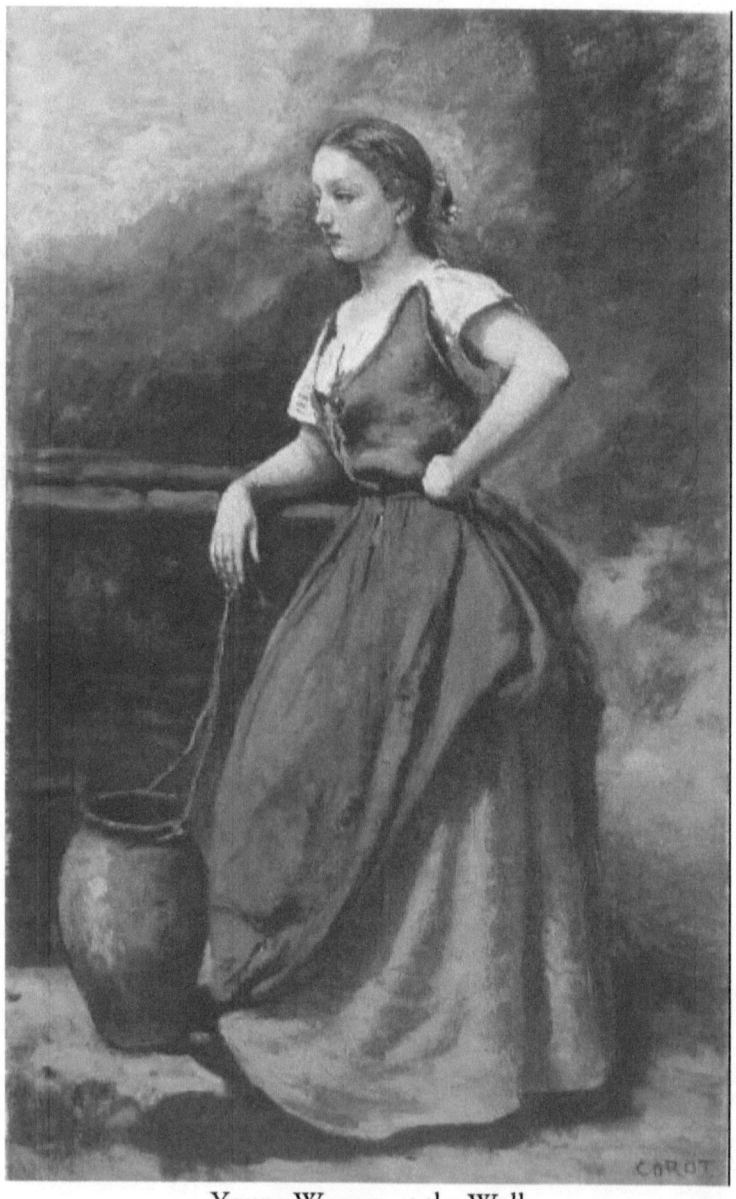

Young Woman at the Well
1870, oil on canvas

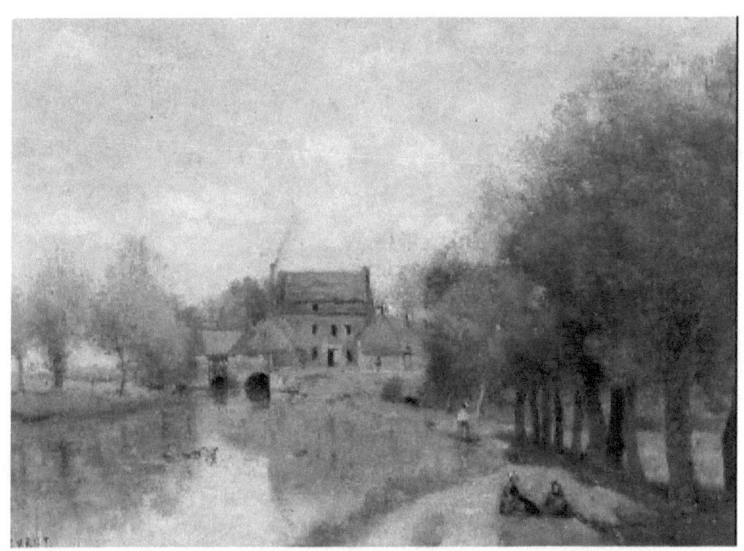

Arleux du Nord, the Drocourt Mill, on the Sensee
1871, oil on canvas

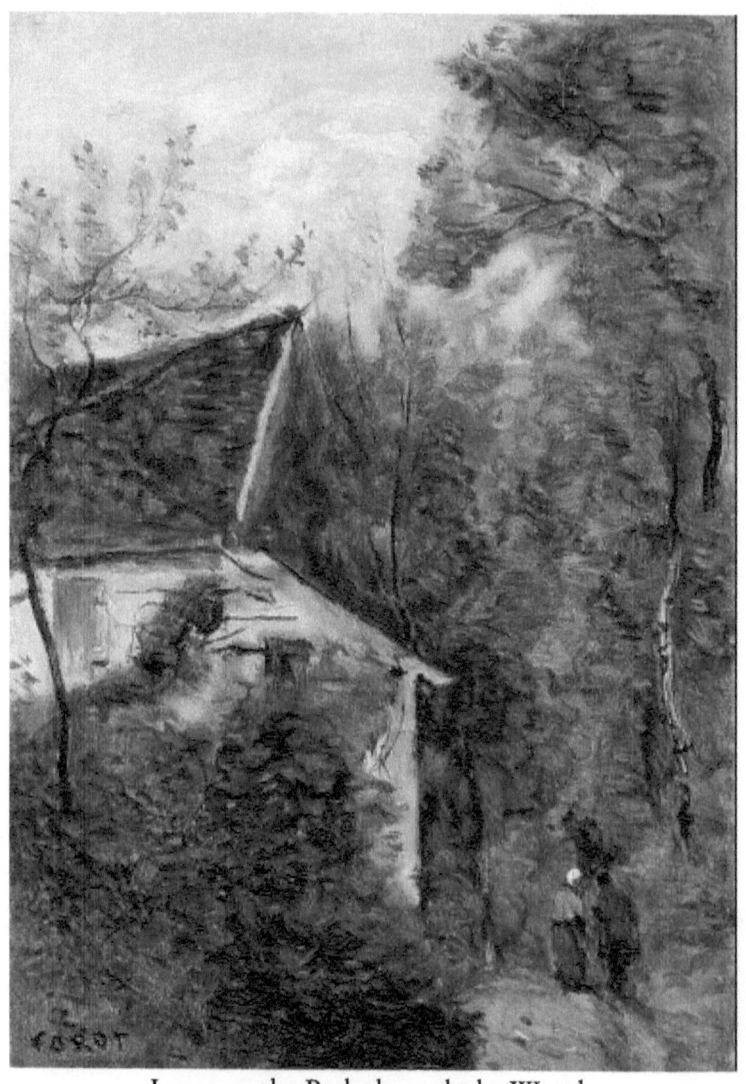

Luzancy, the Path through the Woods
1872, oil on canvas

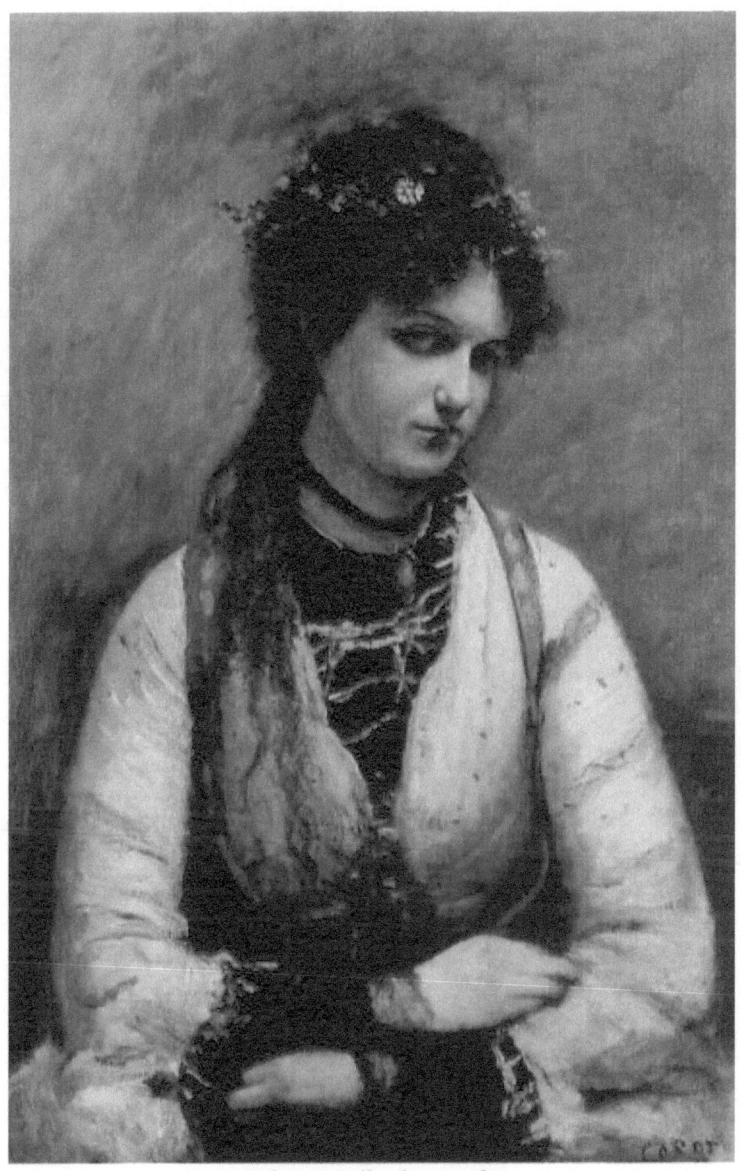

Mademoiselle de Foudras
1872, oil on canvas

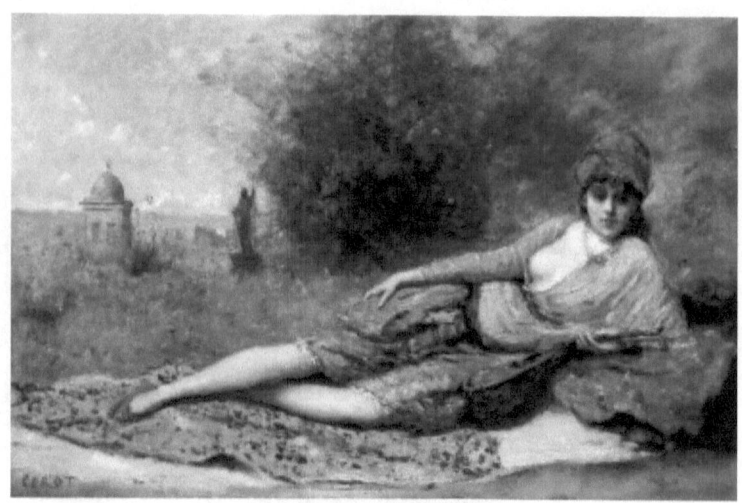

Sicilian Odalisque
1872, oil on canvas

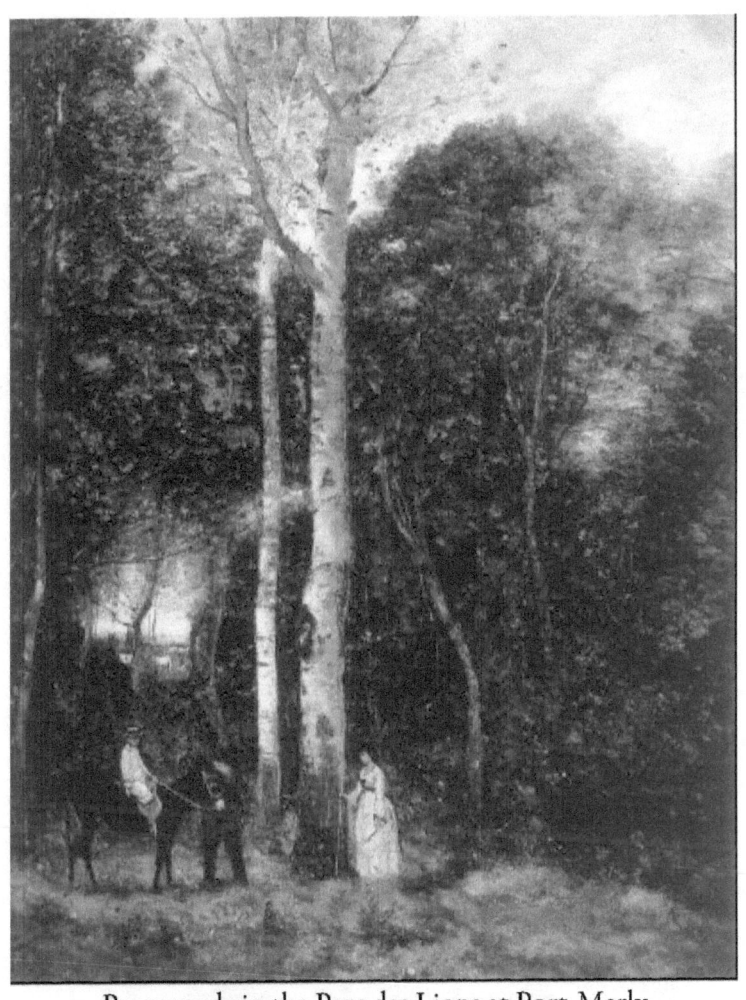

Promenade in the Parc des Lions at Port-Marly
1872, oil on canvas

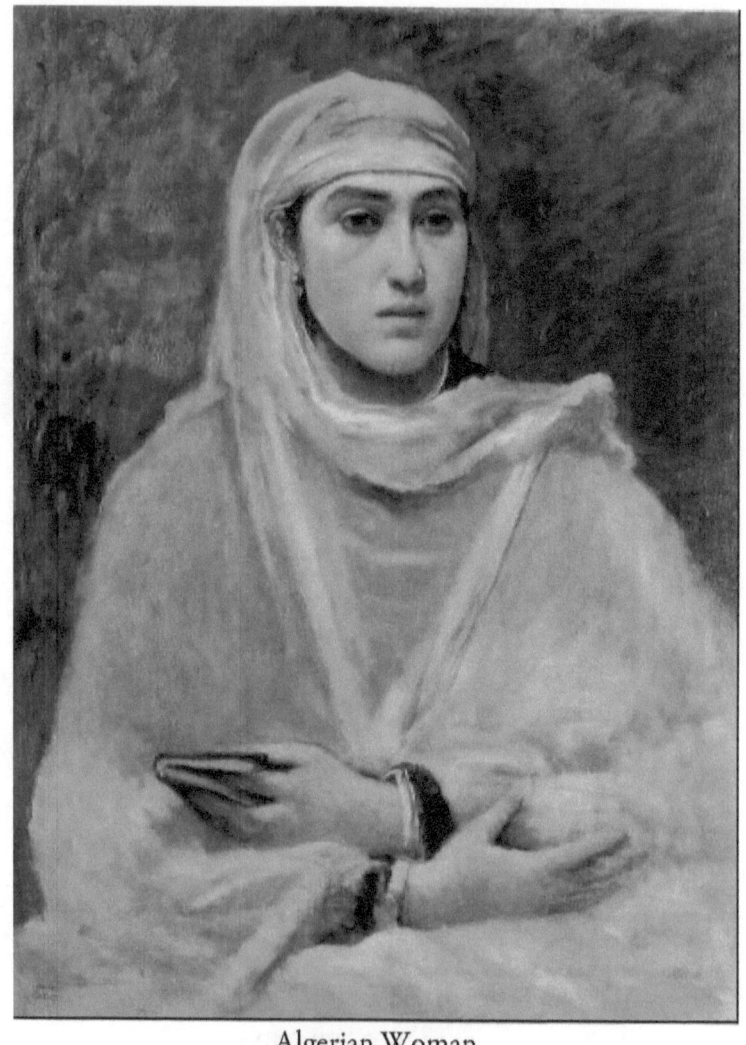

Algerian Woman
1873, oil on canvas

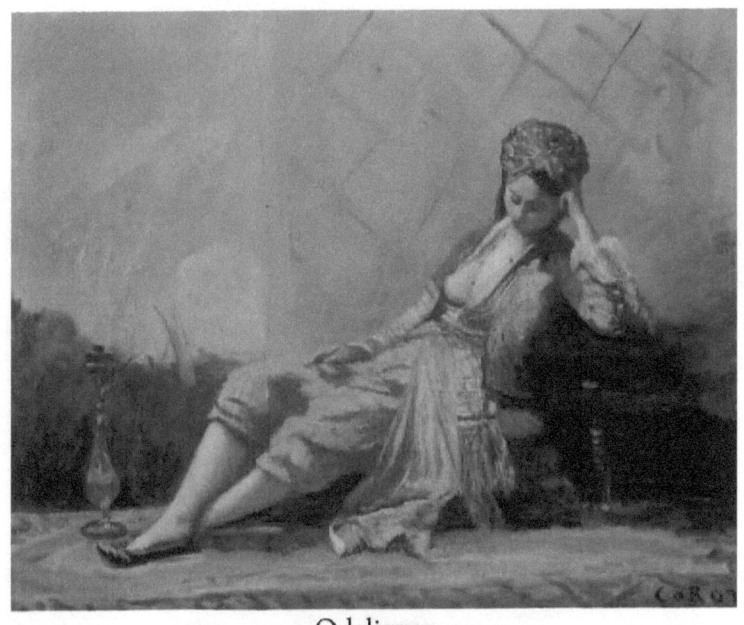

Odalisque
1873, oil on canvas

Maria Tsaneva

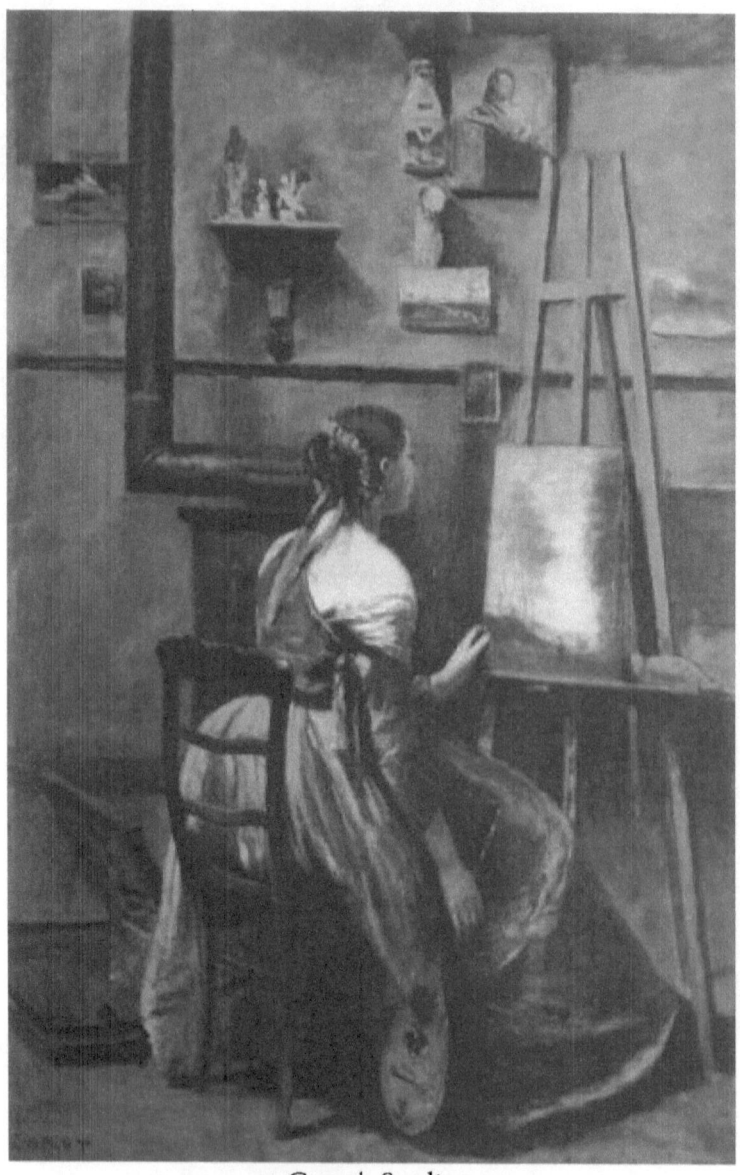

Corot's Studio
c. 1873, oil on canvas

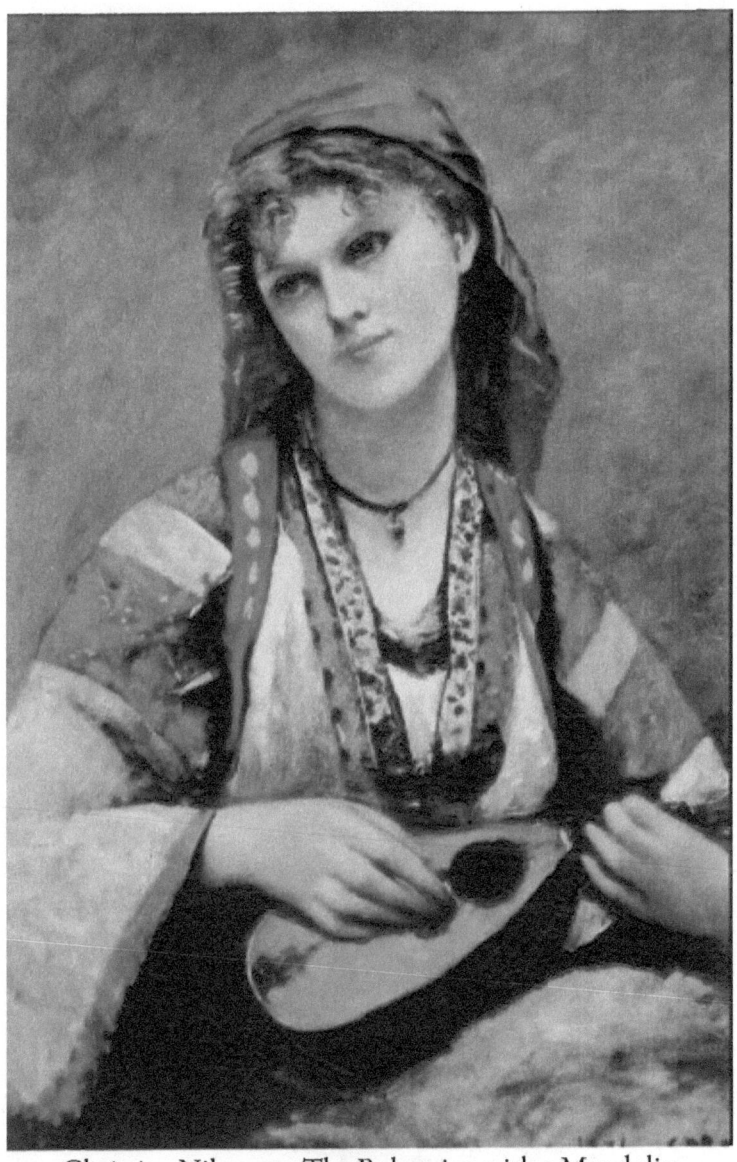

Christine Nilson, or The Bohemian with a Mandolin
1874, oil on canvas

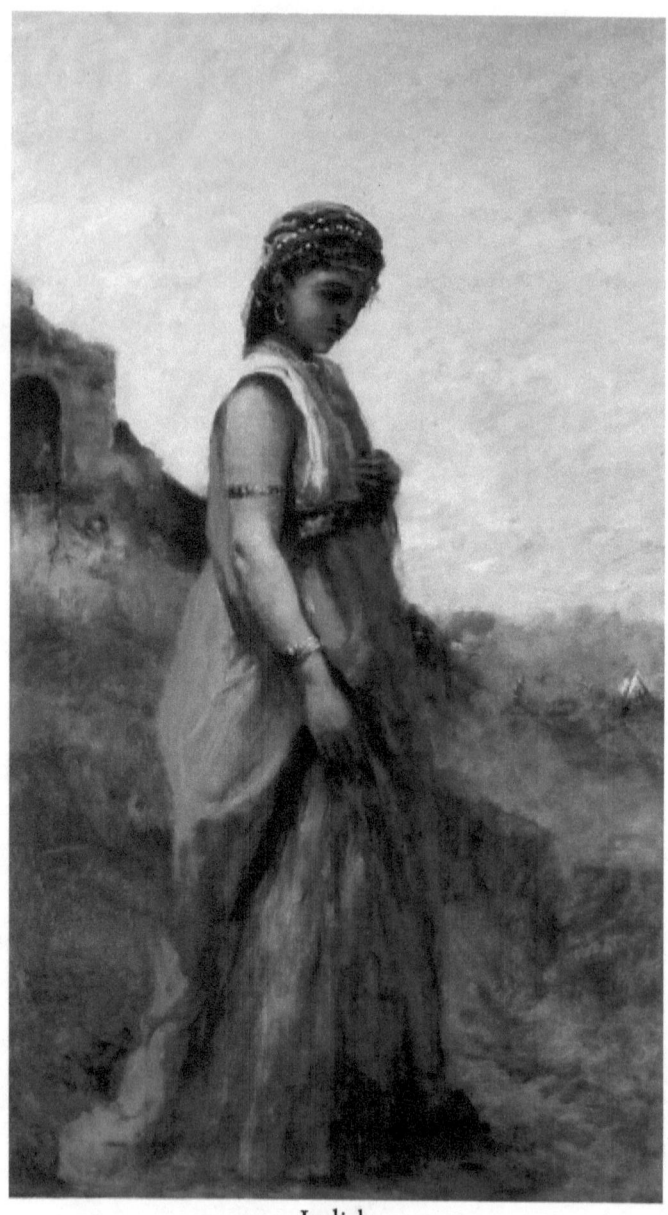

Judith
1874, oil on canvas

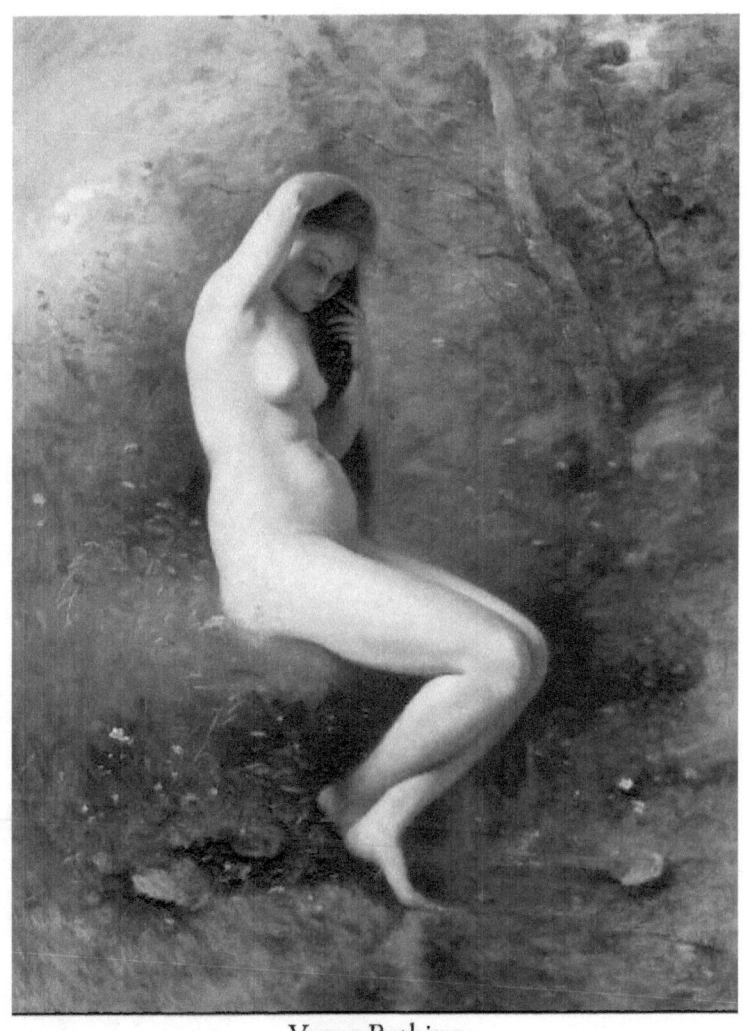

Venus Bathing
1874, oil on canvas

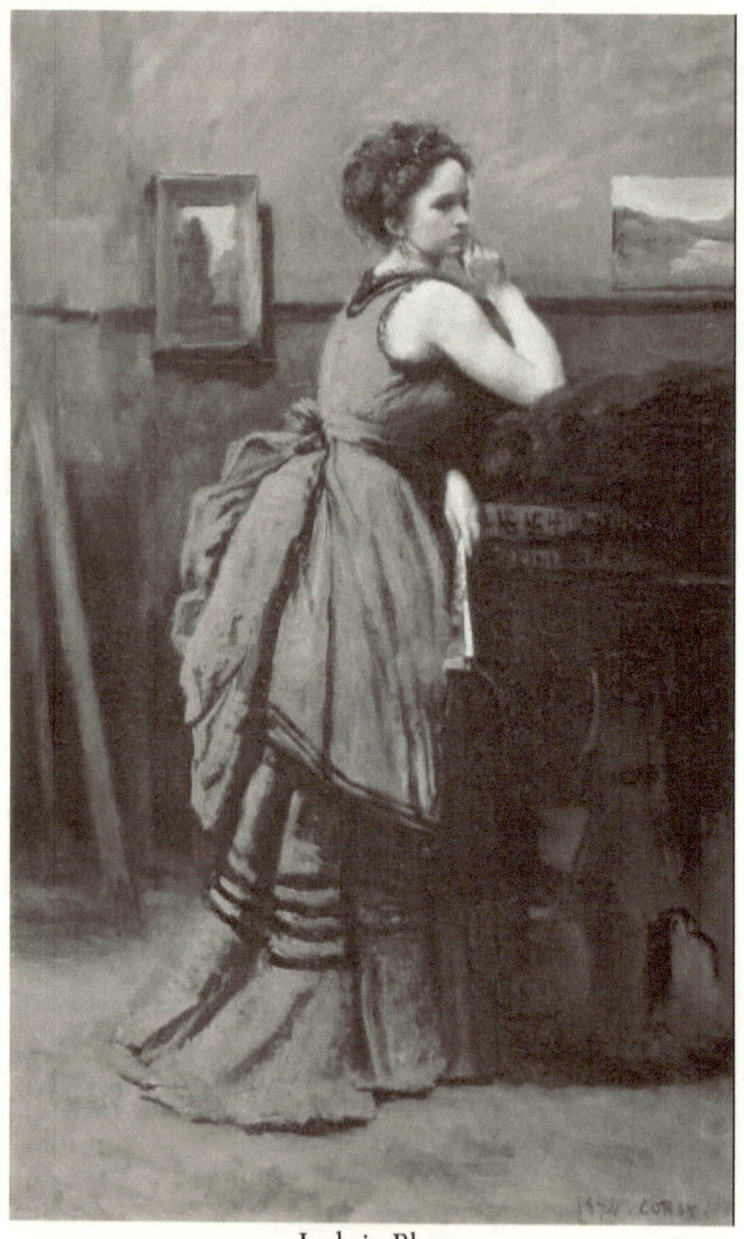

Lady in Blue
1874, oil on canvas

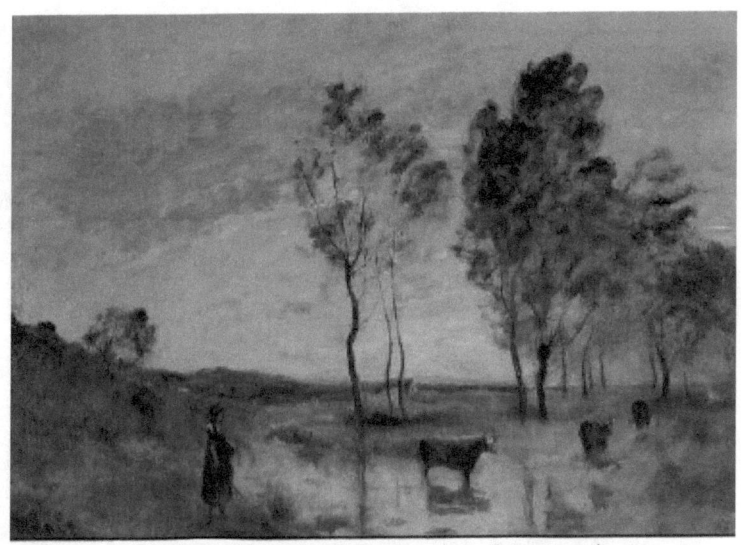

Le Gue (Cows on the Banks of the Gue)
1875, oil on canvas

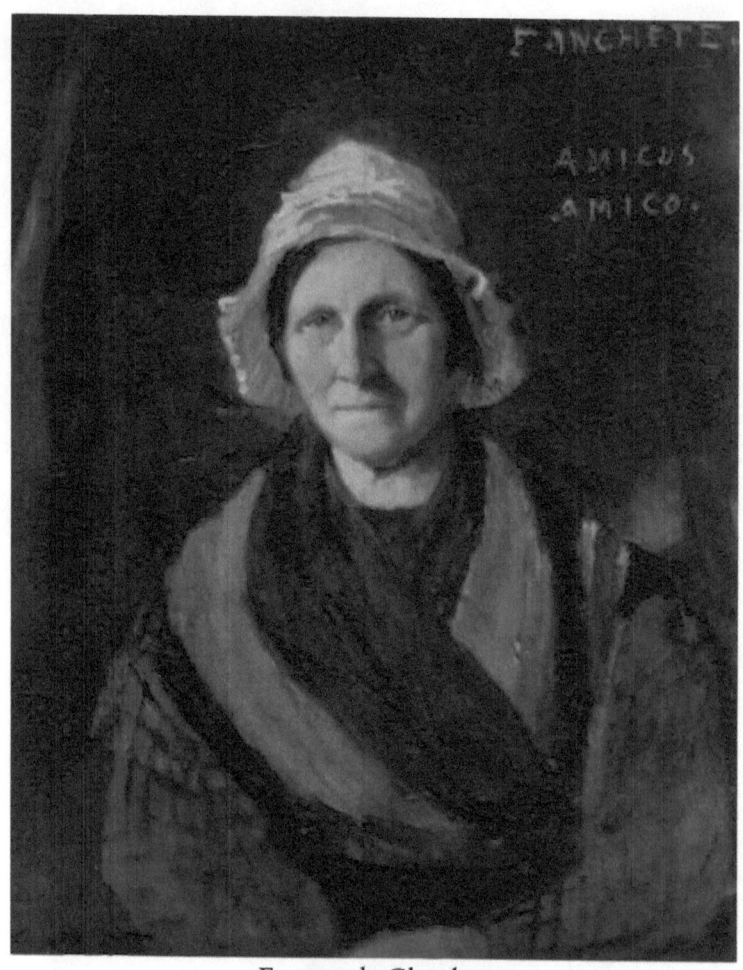

Femme de Chanbre
N.d., oil on canvas

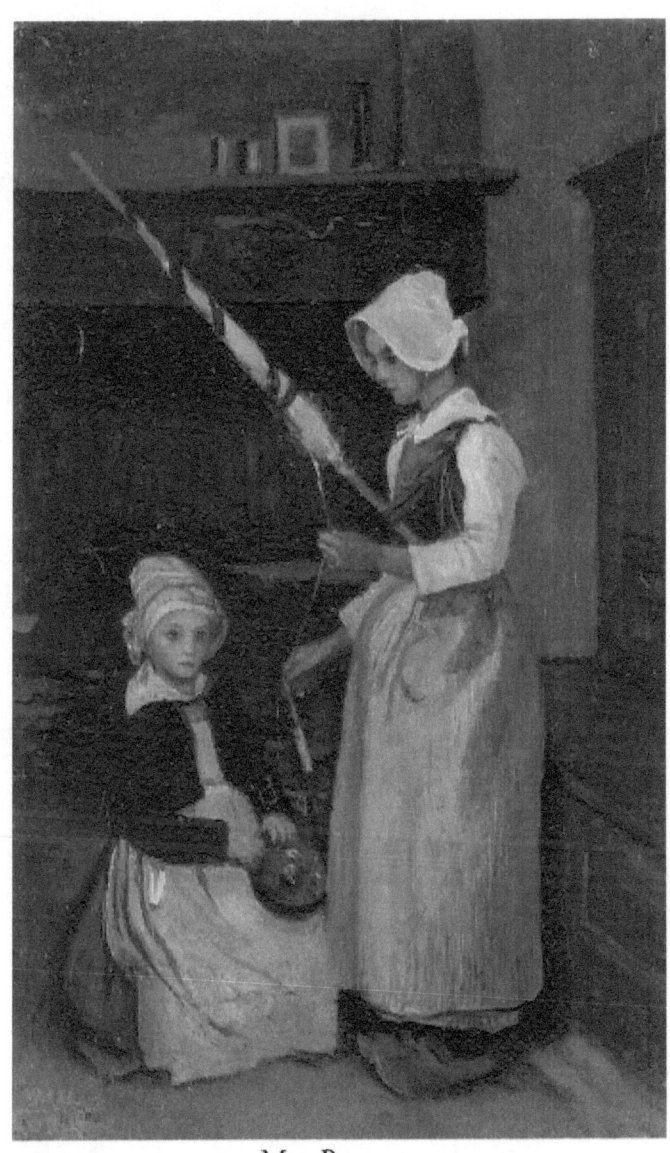

Mur Peasants
N.d., oil on canvas

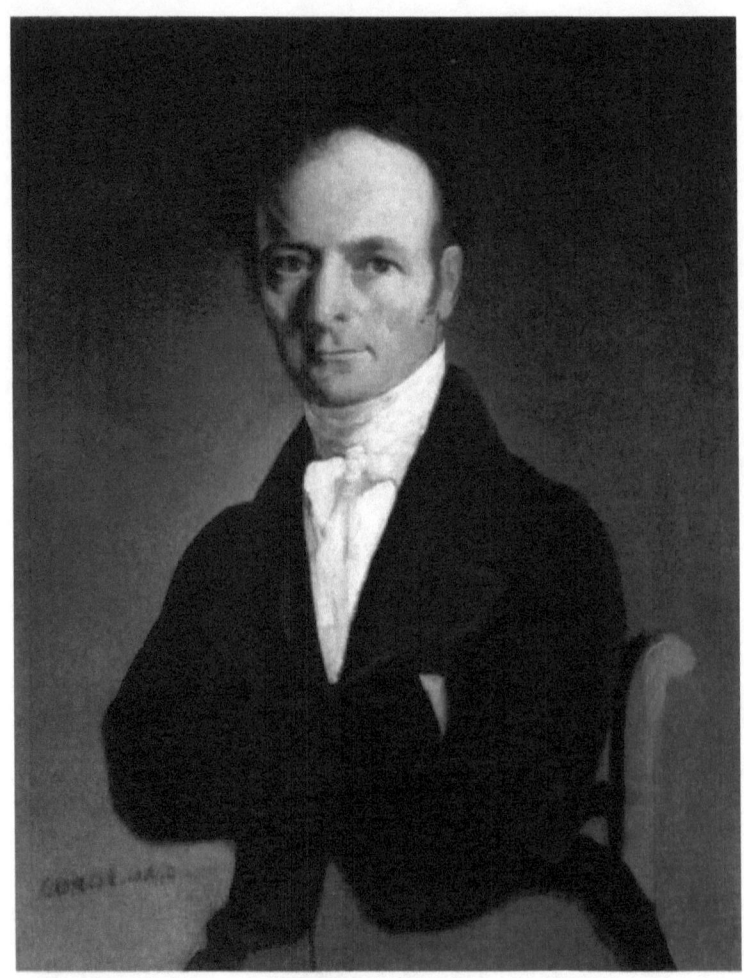

Portrait Of A Man
N.d., oil on canvas

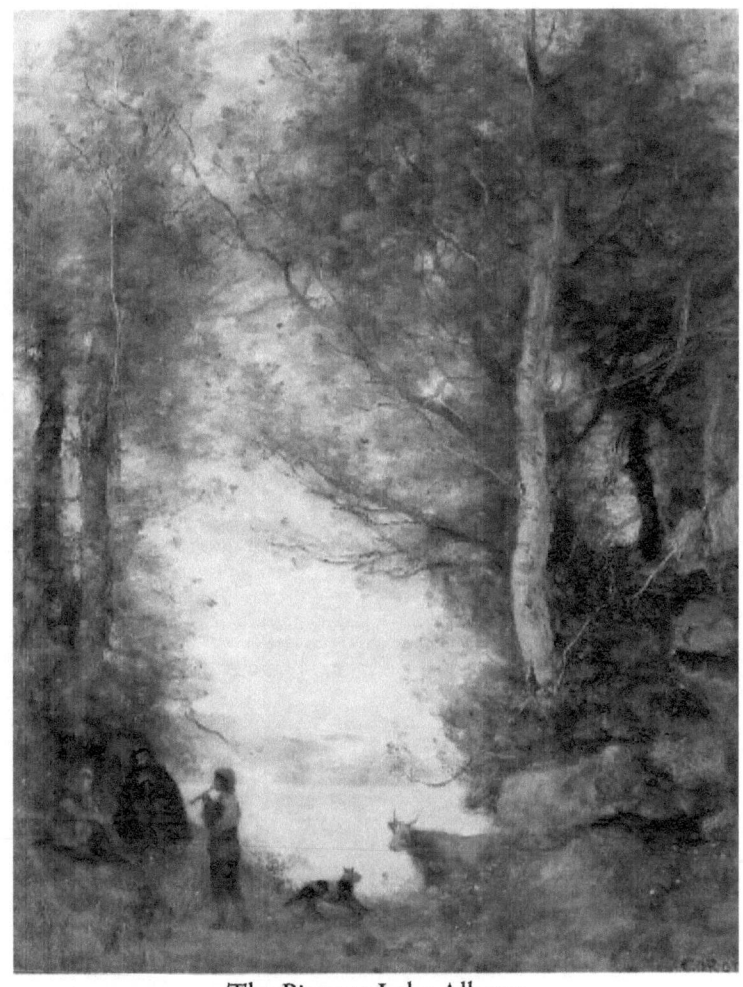

The Piper at Lake Albano
N.d., oil on canvas

Drawings and Etchings

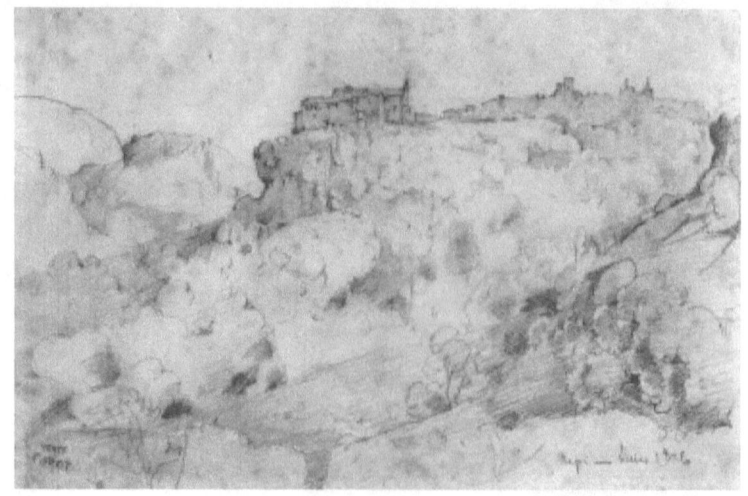

Nepi in Rome
1826, Pencil on white paper

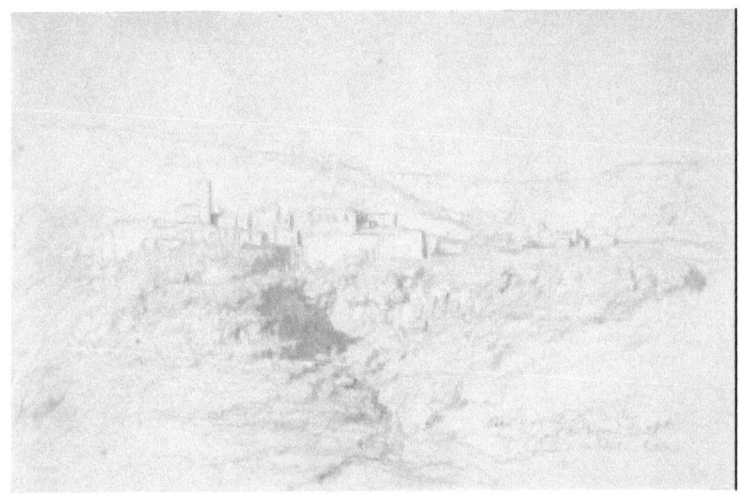

View of Nemi
1826, Graphite on cream wove paper

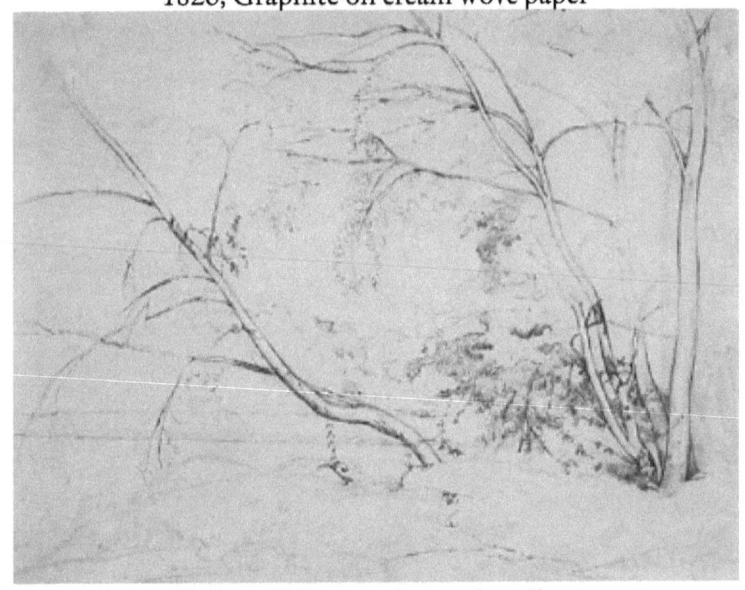

Clump of Trees at Civita Castellana
1826, Graphite on cream wove paper

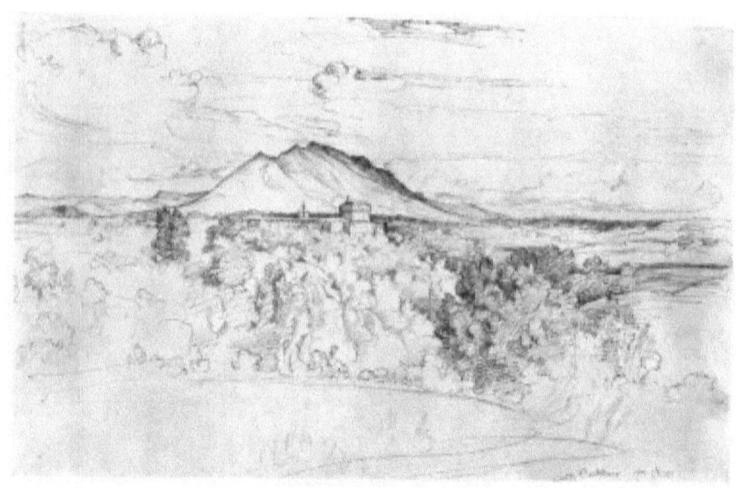

Monte Soracte
1827, Pen and black ink over graphite pencil on white paper

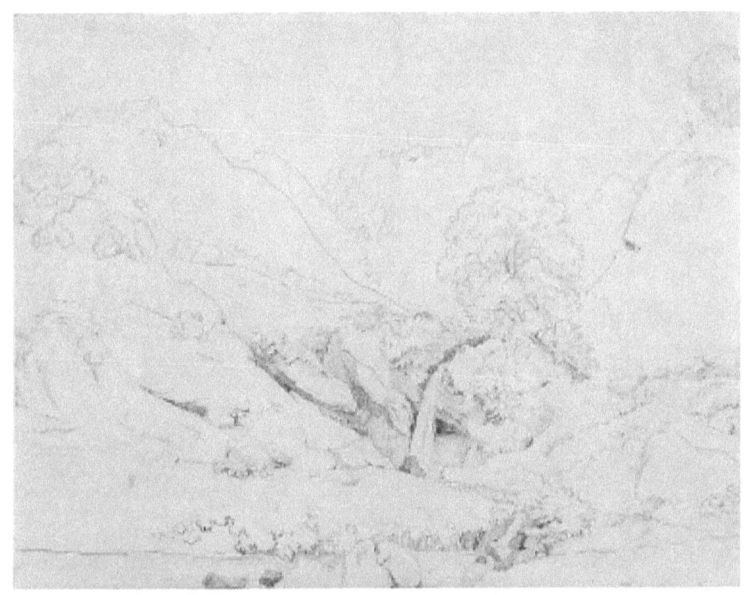

Italian Landscape
1827, Drawing in pen and ink with lead pencil

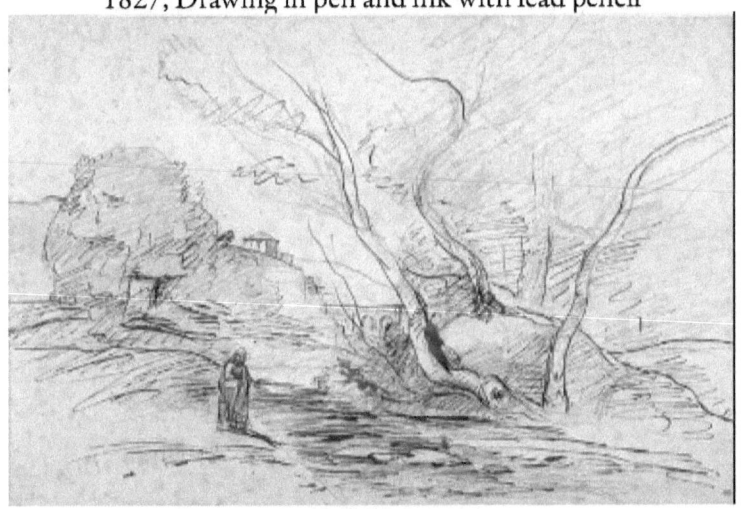

Sketch from nature
1827, Pen and black ink over graphite on paper

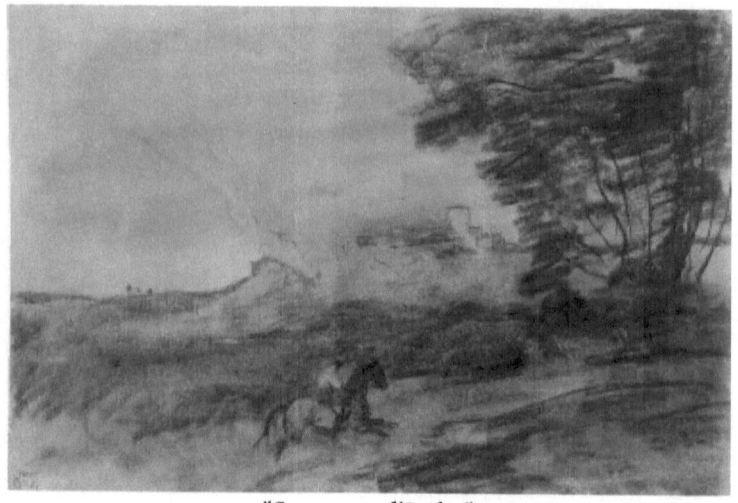

"Souvenir d'Italie"
1830, charcoal on discoloured buff paper, laid down

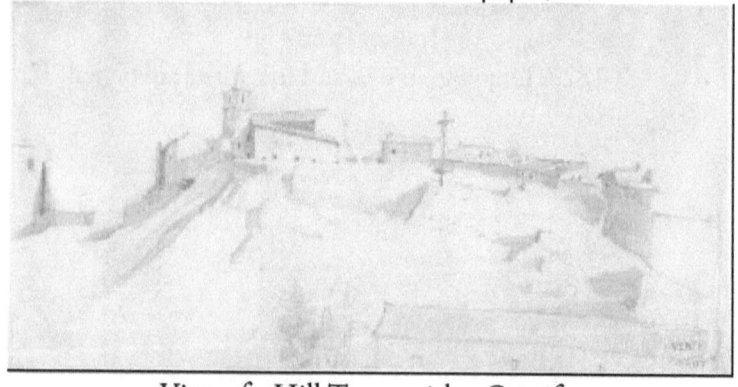

View of a Hill Town with a Crucifix
1830s, Graphite on cream wove paper

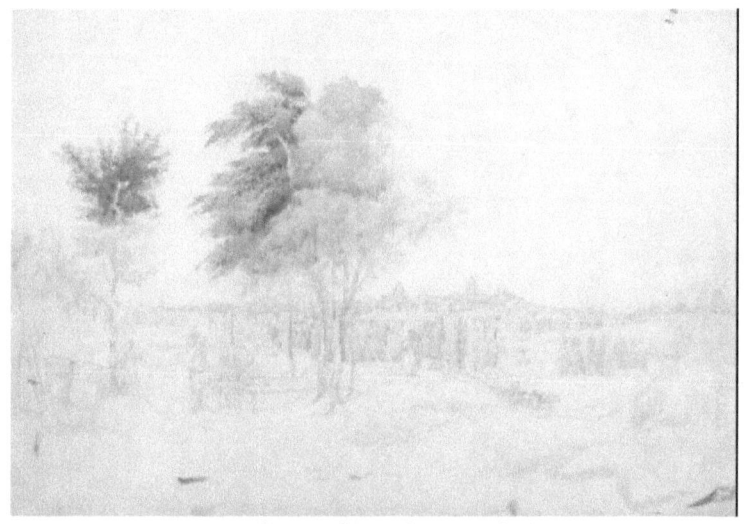

View of Paris from the North-East
1830-35, graphite and watercolor

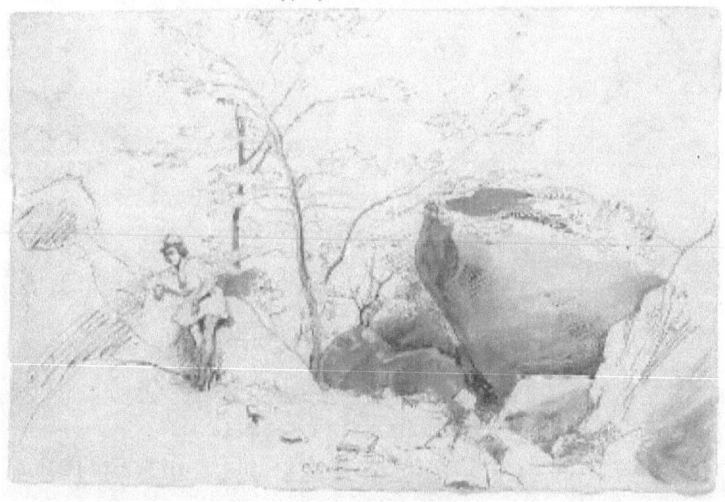

Fontainebleau, Figure Leaning Against a Rock
1830-35, Pen and brown ink, brush and brown wash over
pencil on paper

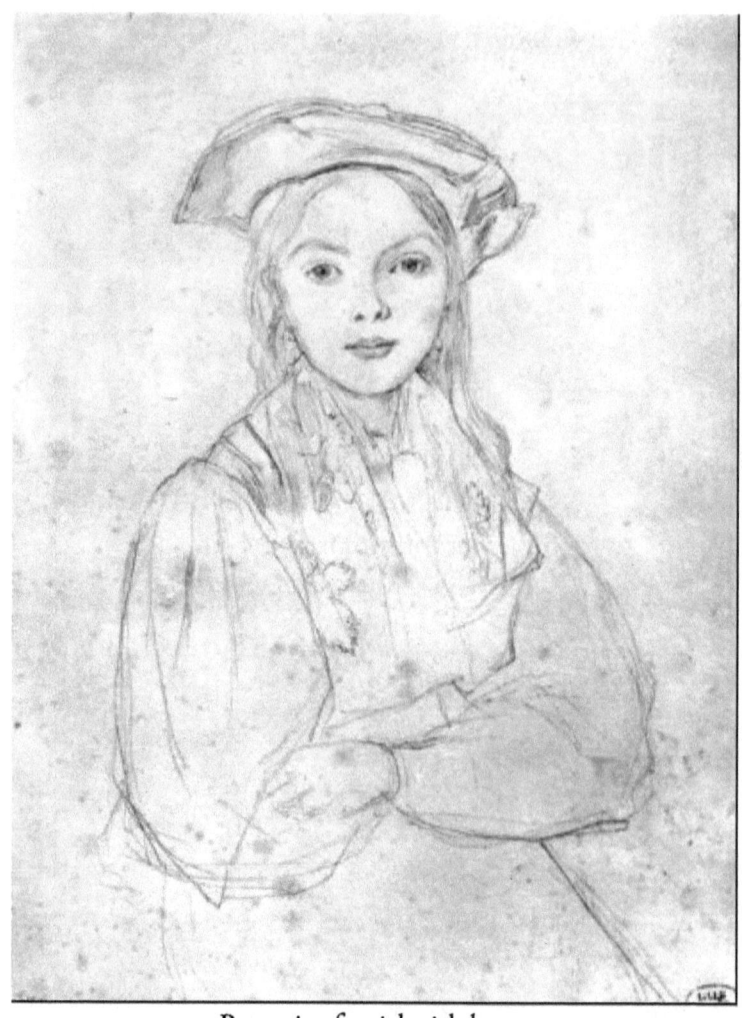

Portrait of a girl with beret
1831, Pen and black ink over graphite on white paper

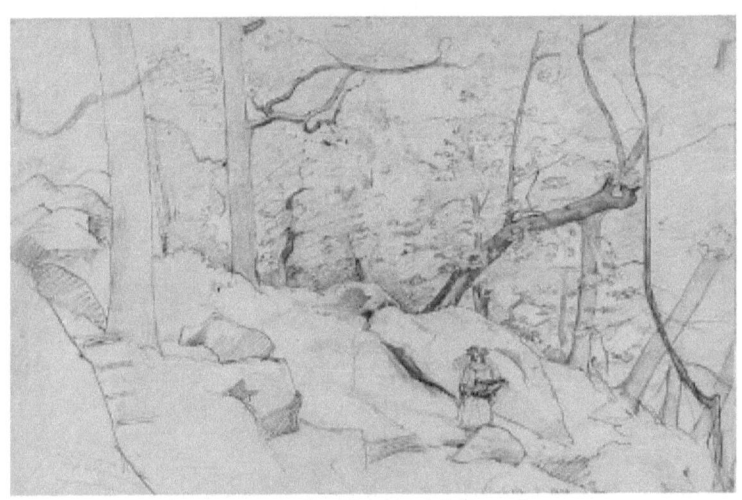

Painters in the Fontainebleau forest
1833, Drawing in pen and ink with lead pencil

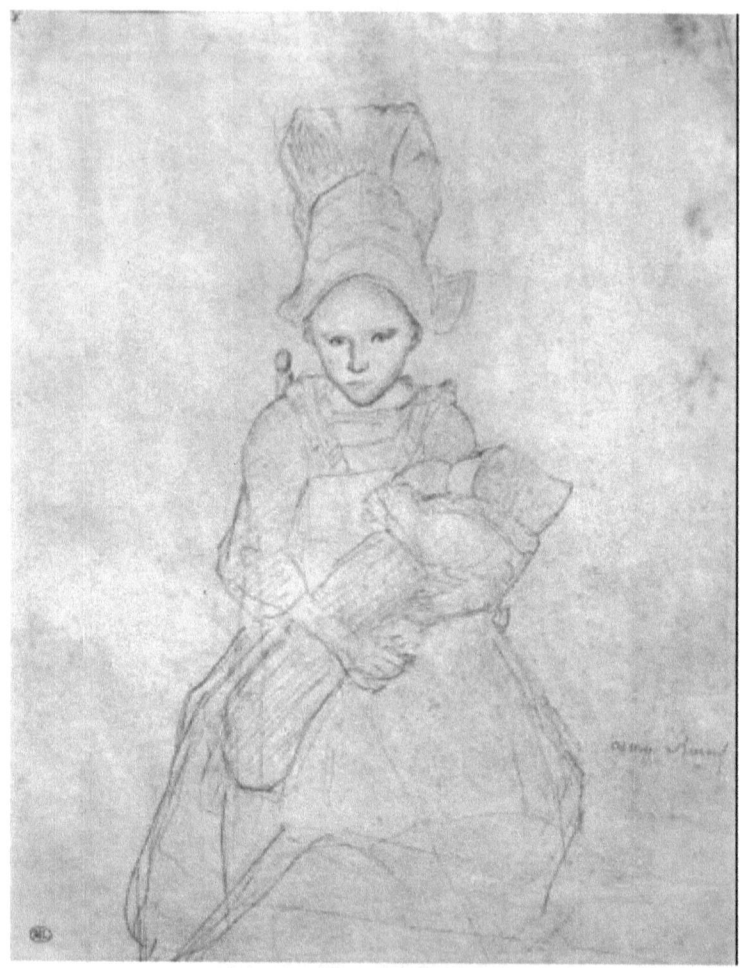

Portrait of a child with doll
1835, Pencil on white paper

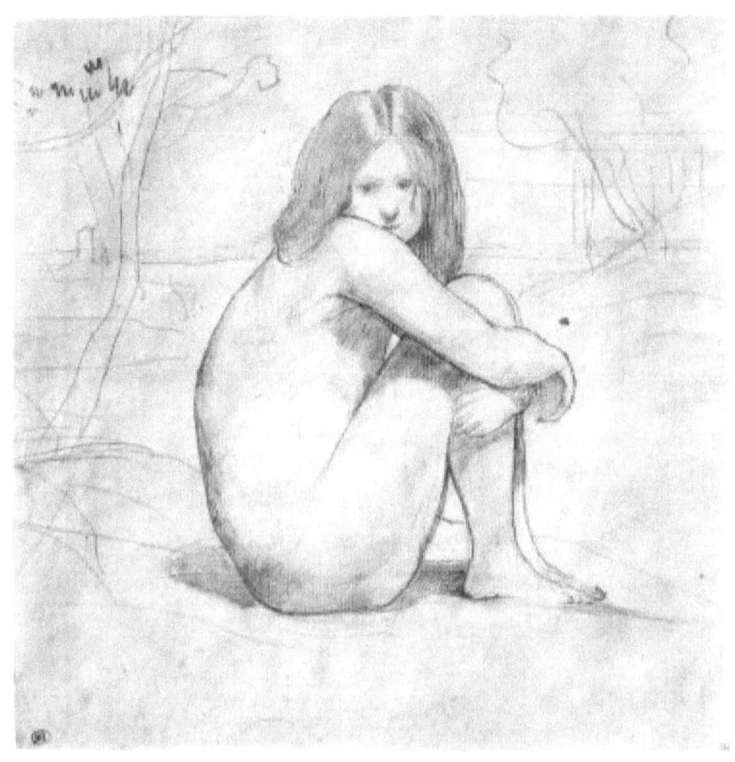

Nude Girl in Landscape
1835–1840, Pencil, pen and black ink, on paper

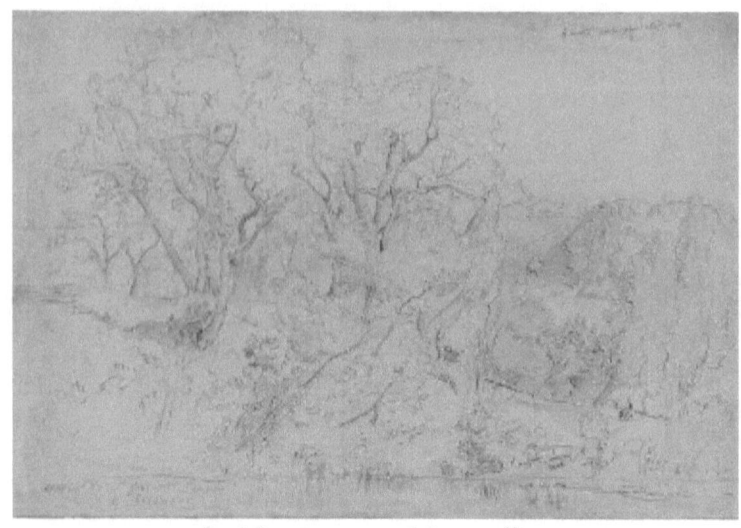

Le Martinet near Montpellier
1836, Pen and black ink, graphite on light blue laid paper

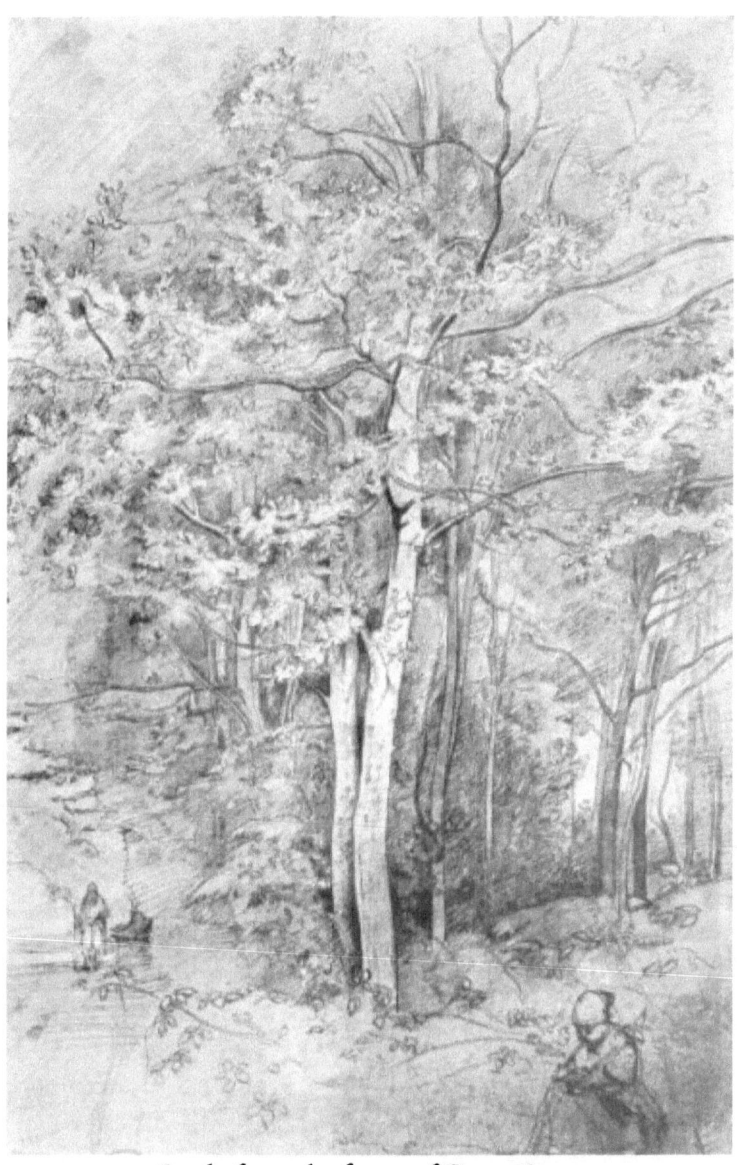

Study from the forest of Compiègne
1840, Chalk, pen and black ink, on white paper

Maria Tsaneva

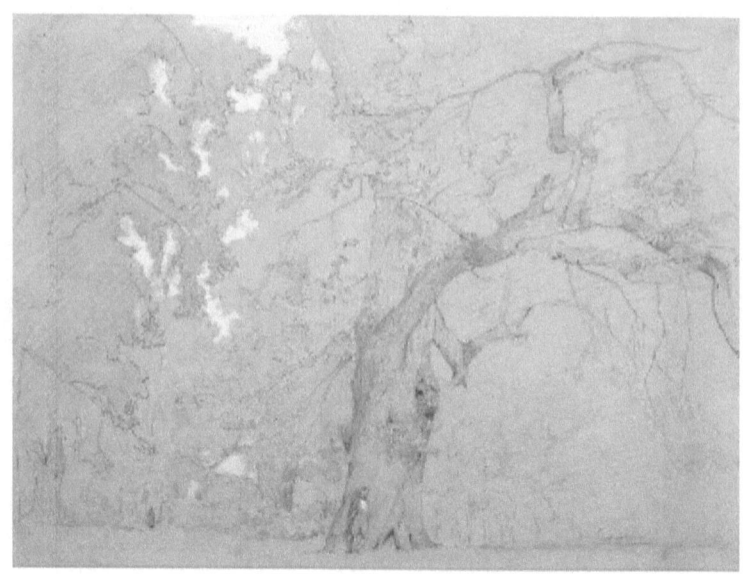

Young Man in front of a Great Oak
1840-1842, Graphite heightened with white gouache on tan
paper

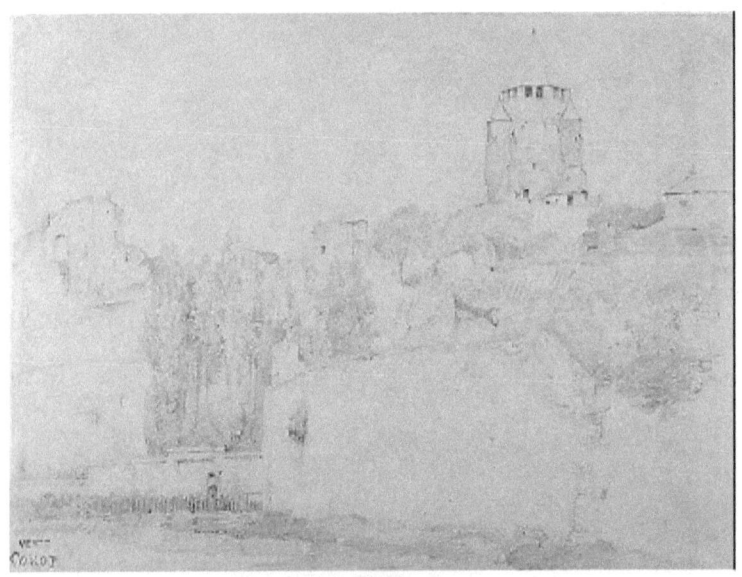

View of Provins
1842, Pencil on white wove paper

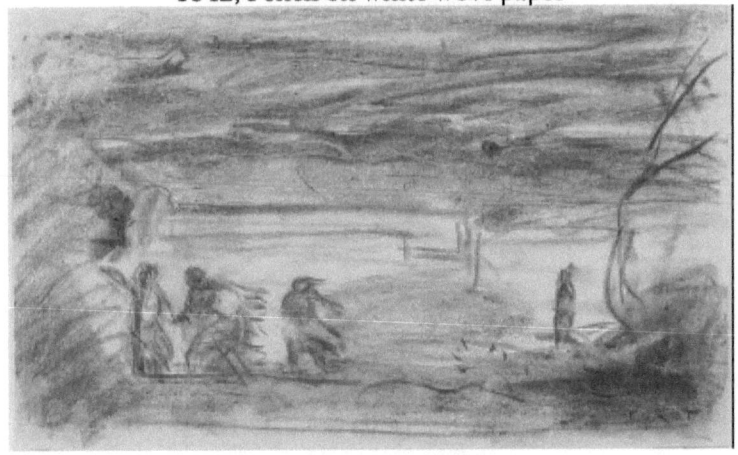

The destruction of Sodom
1844, charcoal on light brown paper

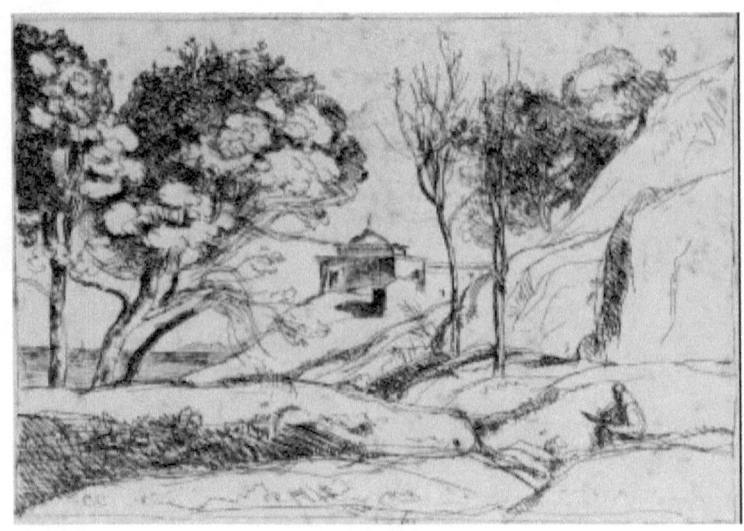

Memories of Tuscany
1845, etching

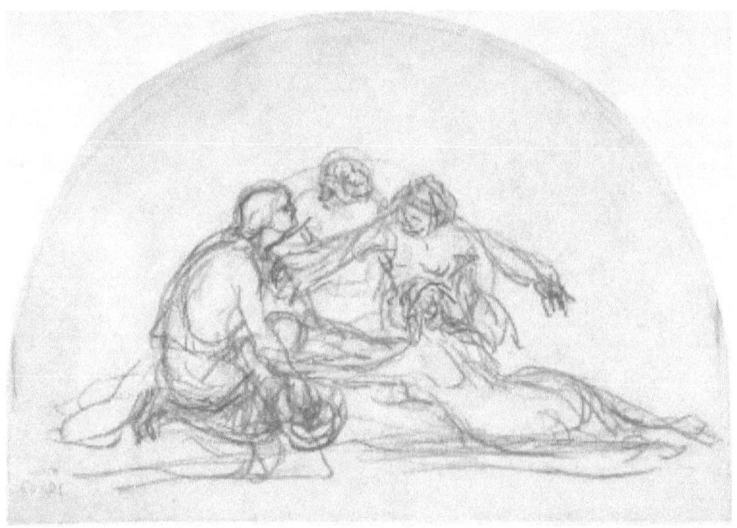

Three Nymphs and a Youth: study for a decorative lunette
1850, Black chalk and graphite on laid paper (trimmed in the
shape of an arch)

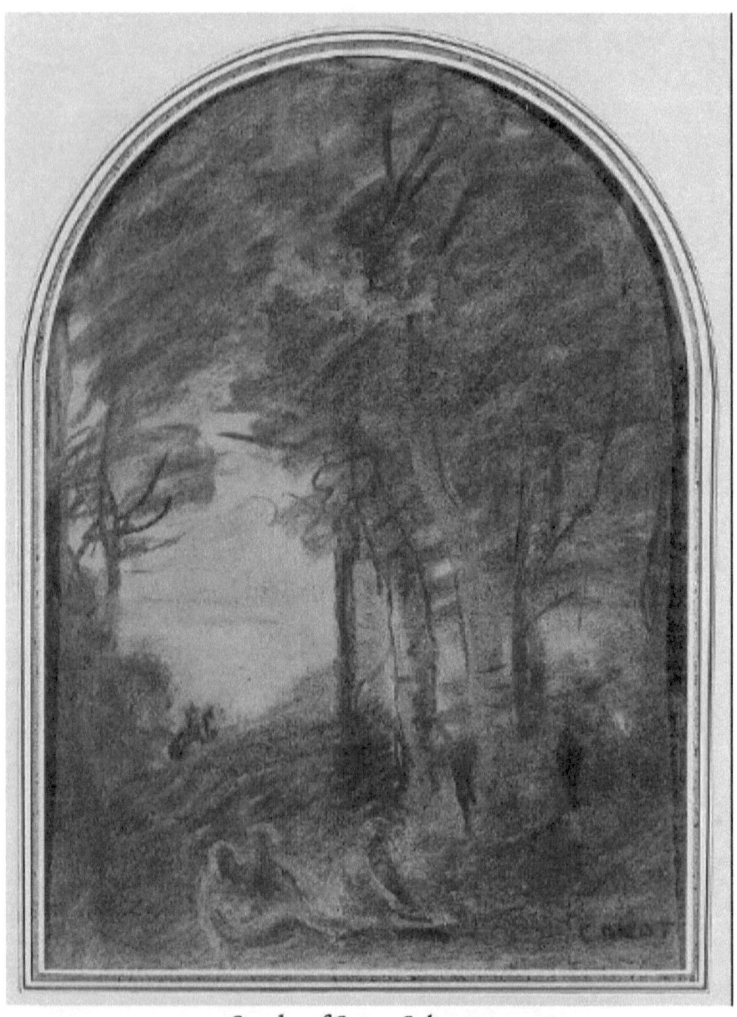

Study of Saint Sebastian
1852, charcoal on rough, moderately-thick, brown wove paper

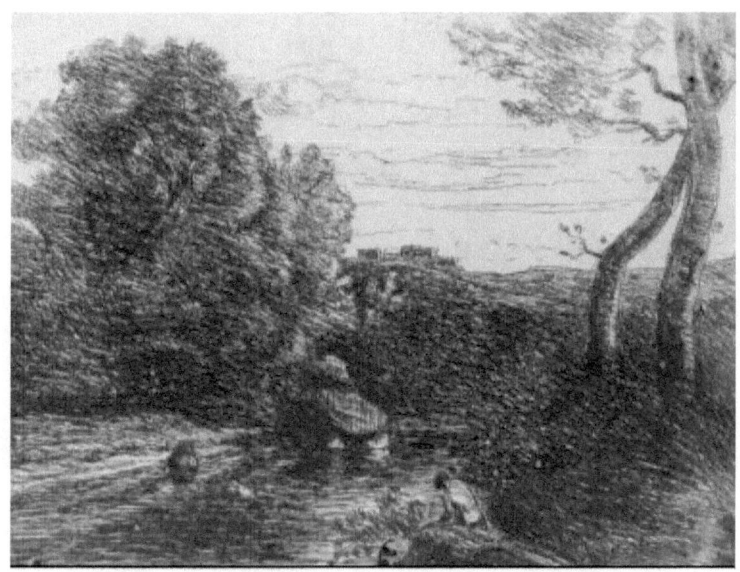

The bath of the Shepherd
1853, etching

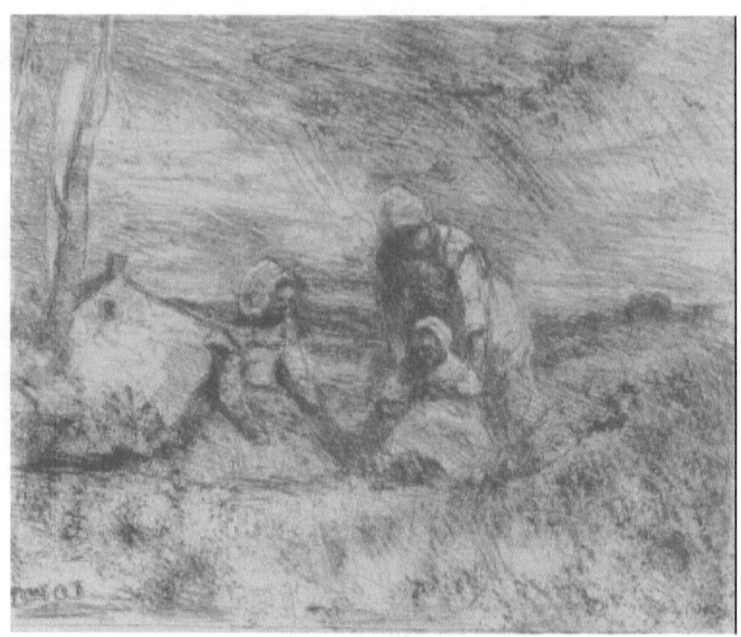

The Little Sister
1854, etching

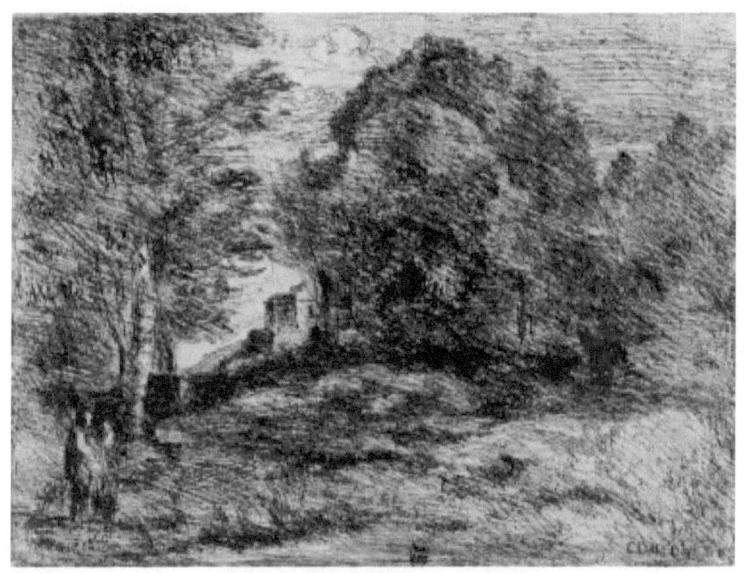

The grave of Sémiramis
1854, etching

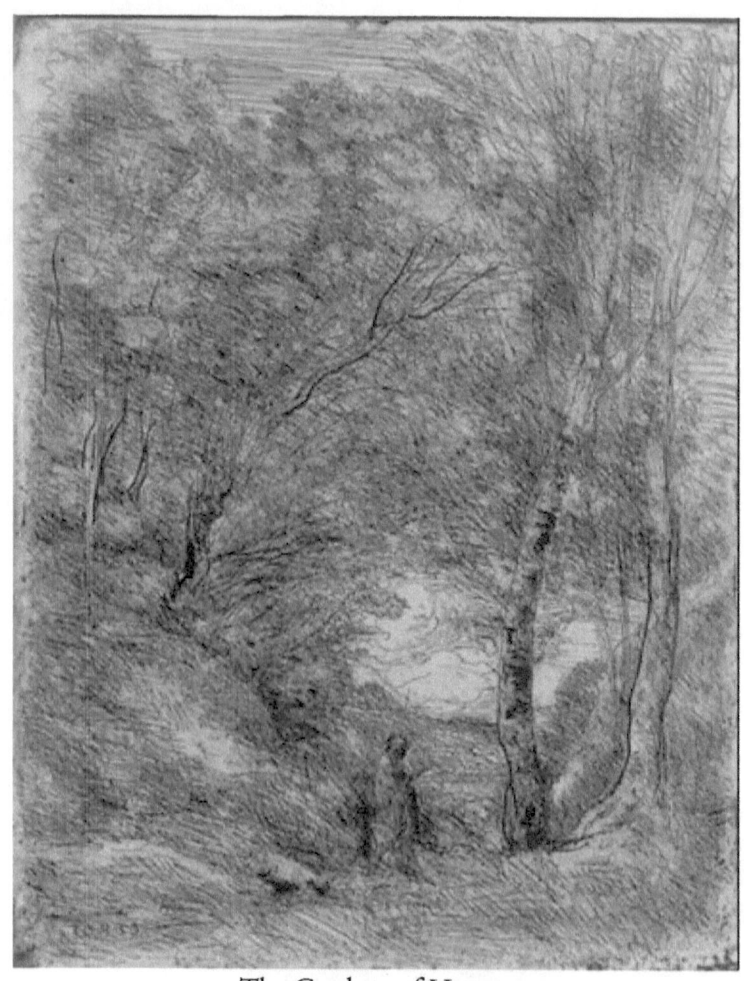

The Gardens of Horace
1855, etching on wove paper

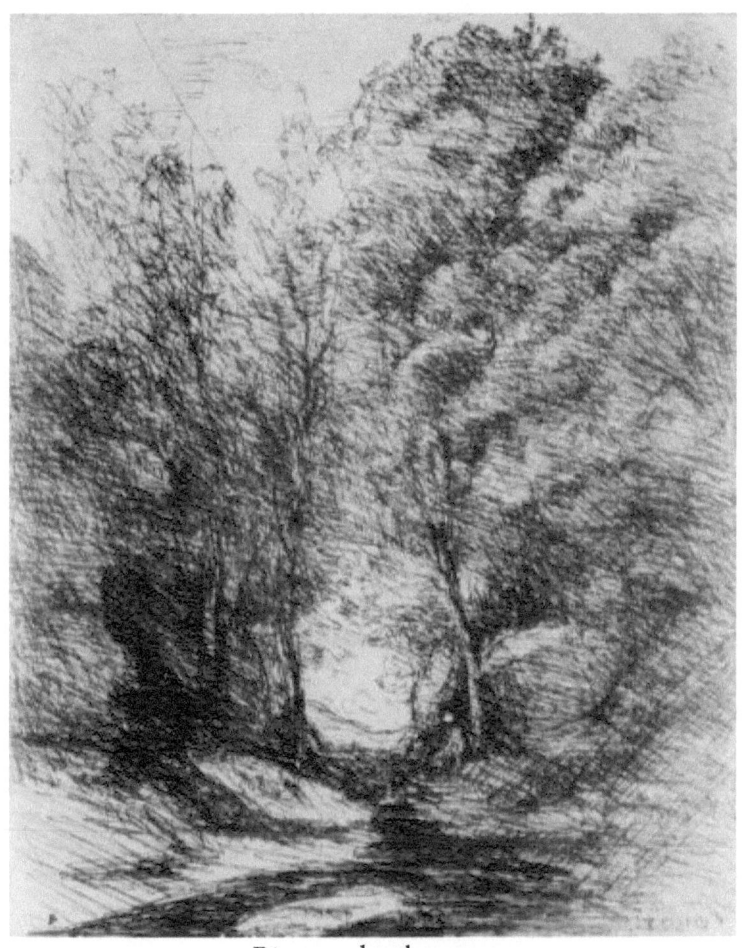

River under the trees
1855, etching

Maria Tsaneva

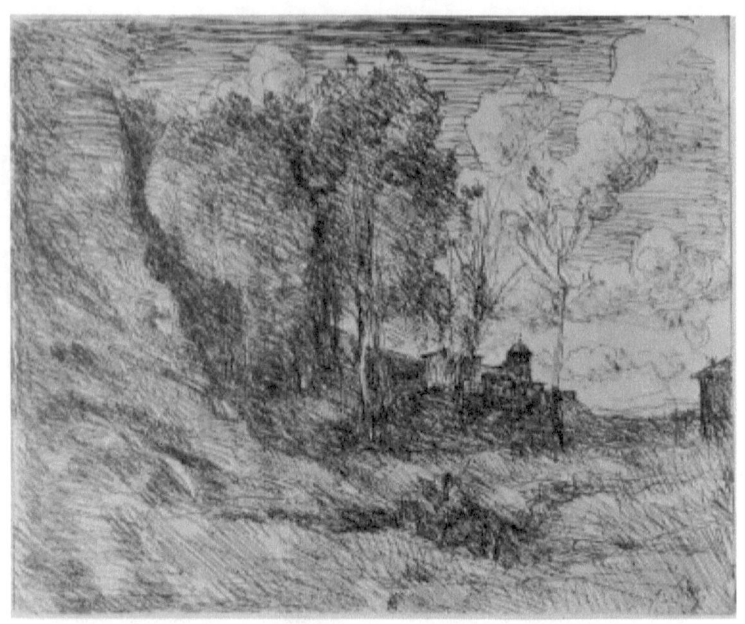

Memory of Ostie
1855, etching

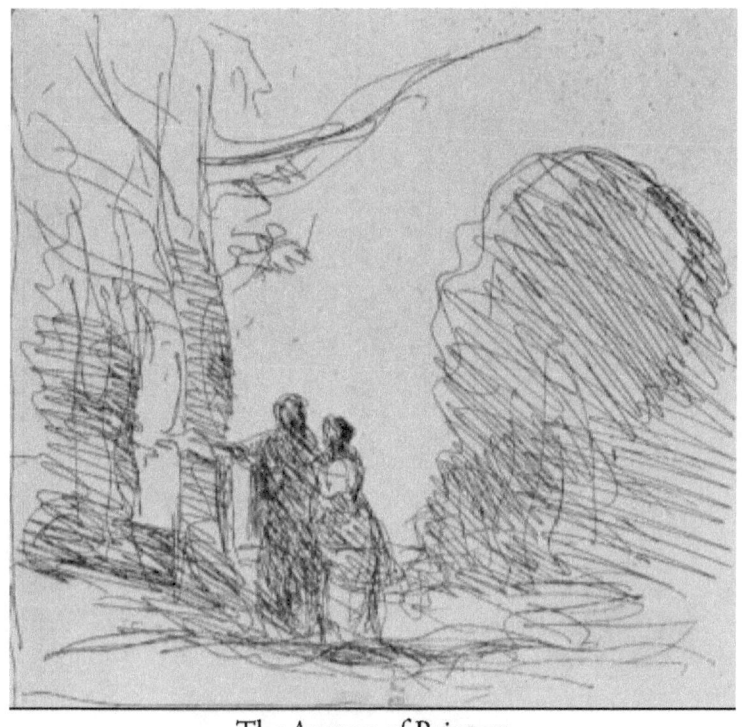

The Avenue of Painters
1856, etching

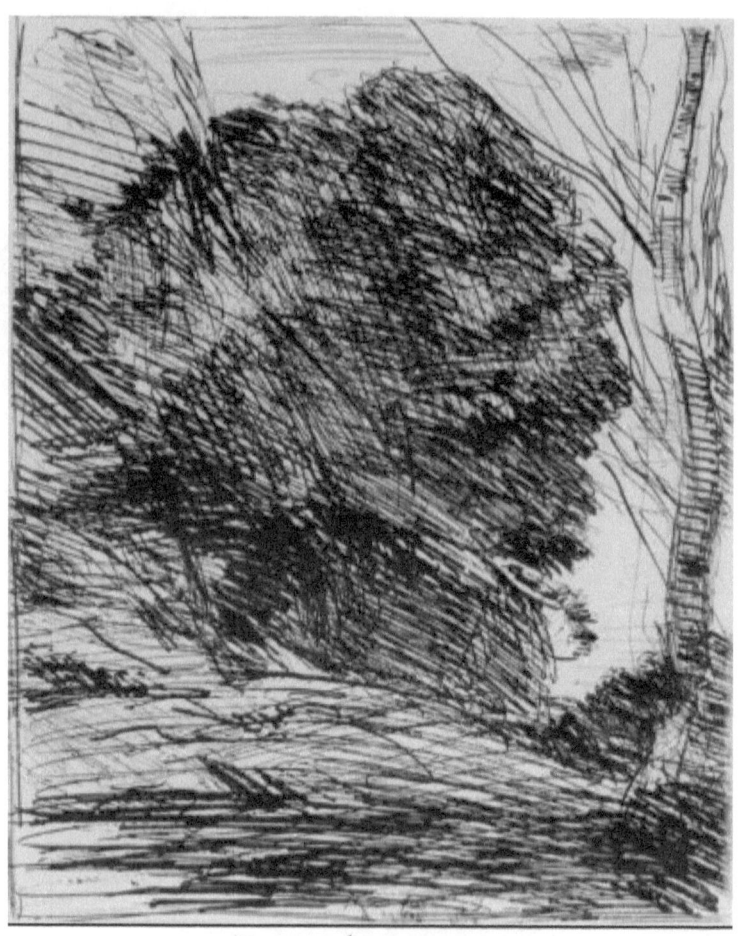

Trees in the mountains
1856, etching

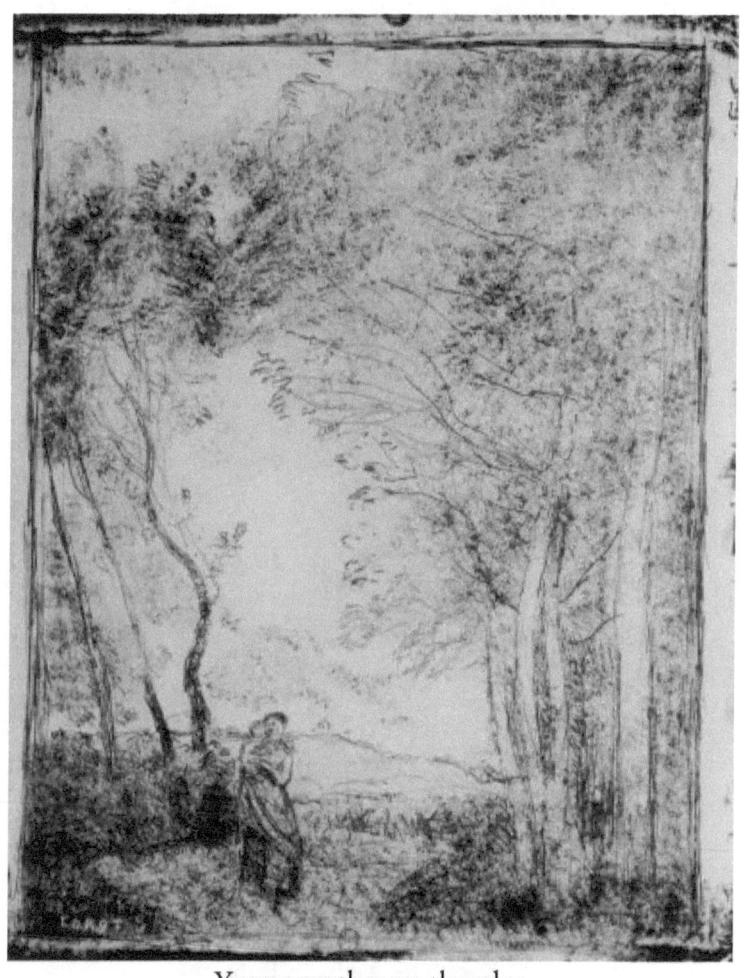

Young mother on the edge
1856, etching

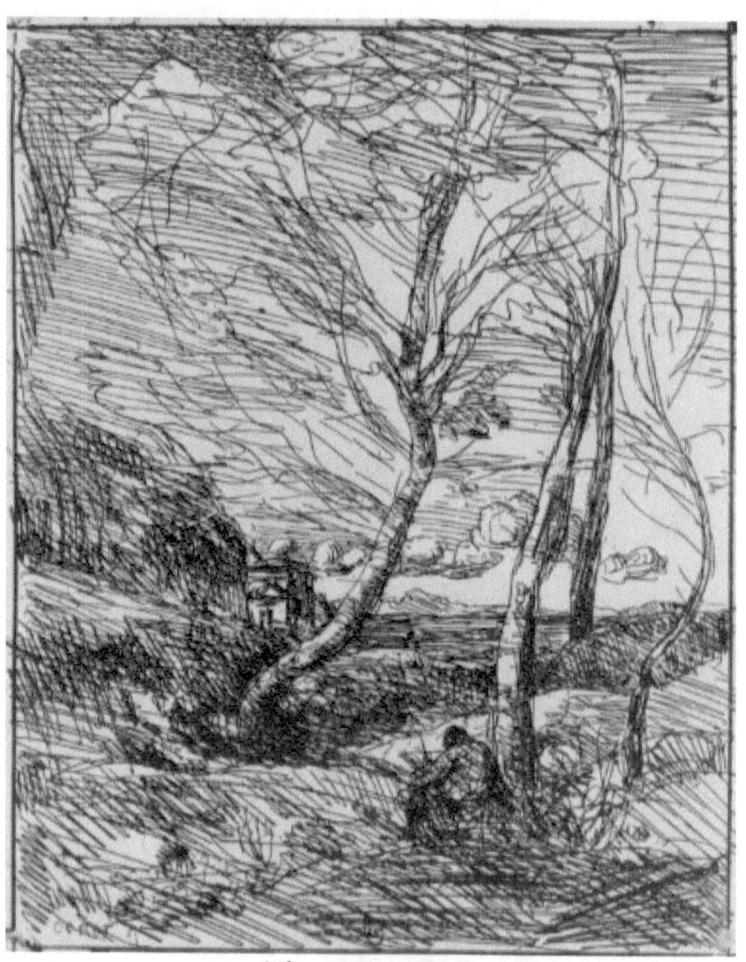

The Artist in Italy
1857, etching

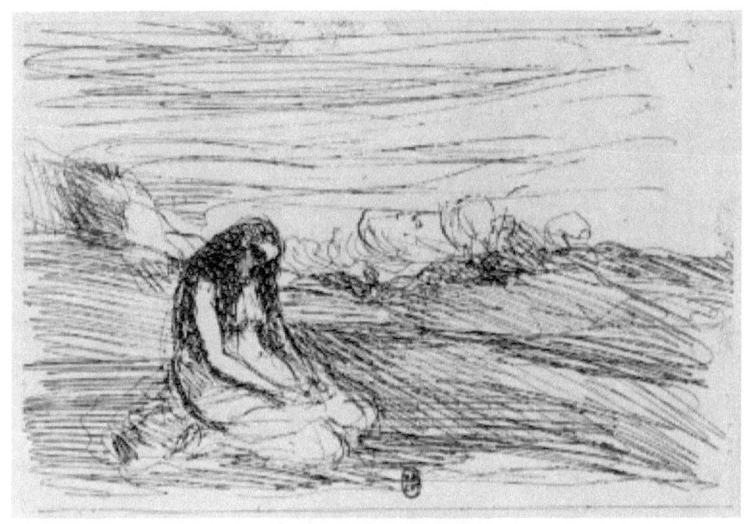

Praying Magdalena
1858, etching

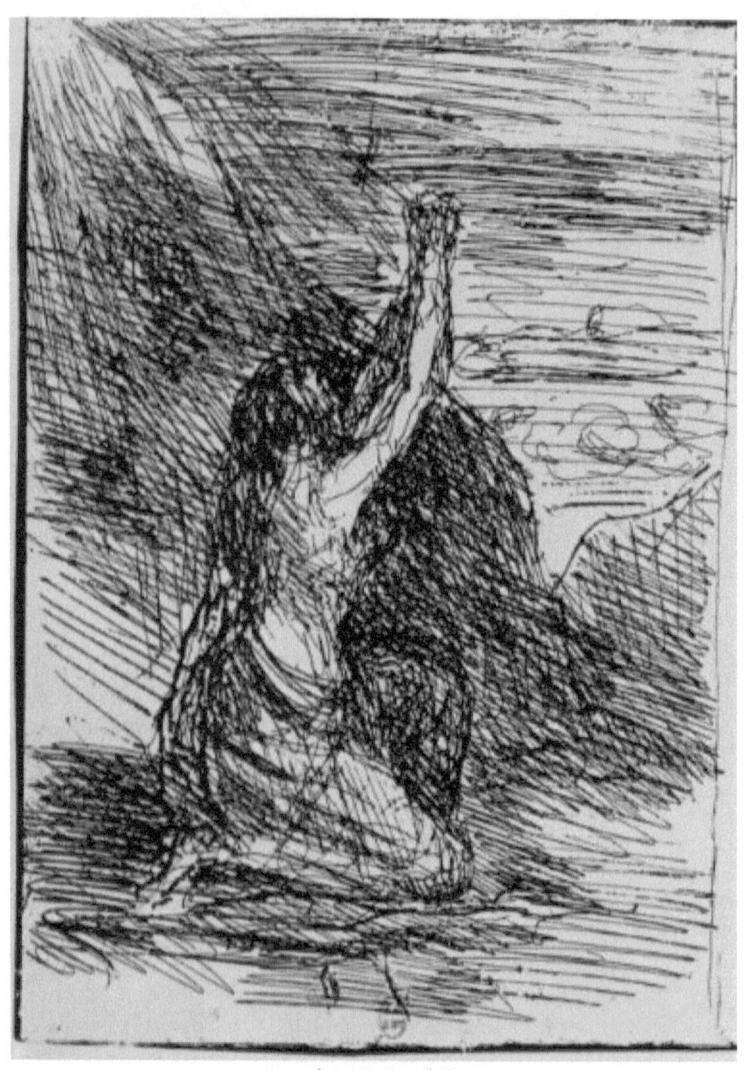

Kneeling Magdalene
1858, etching

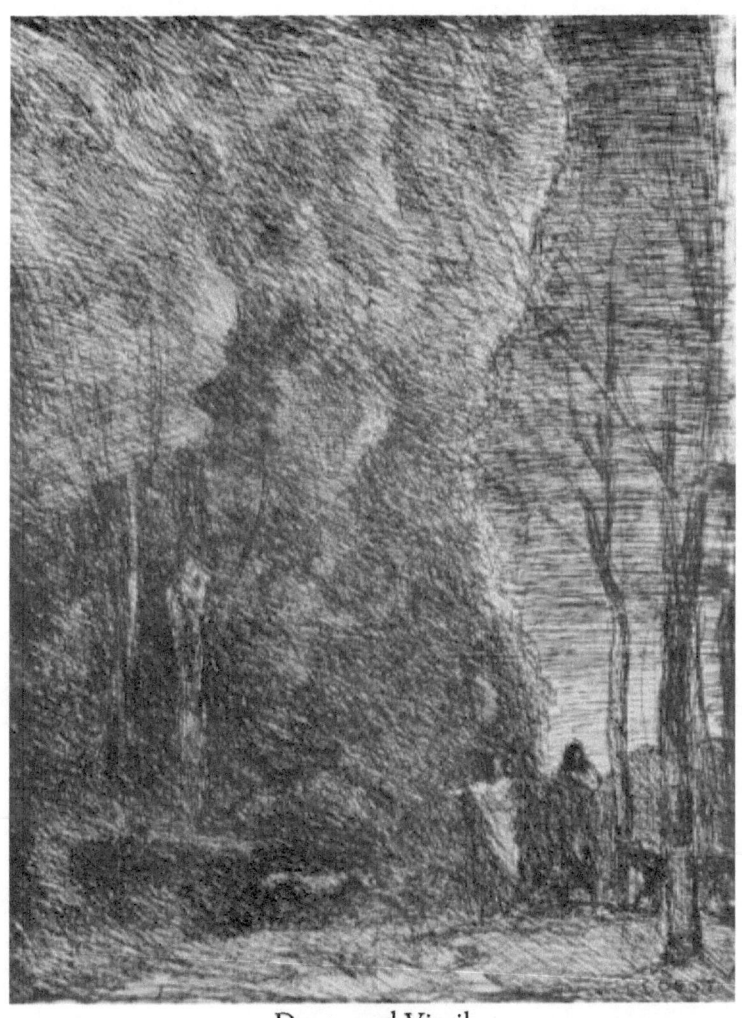

Dante and Virgil
1858, etching

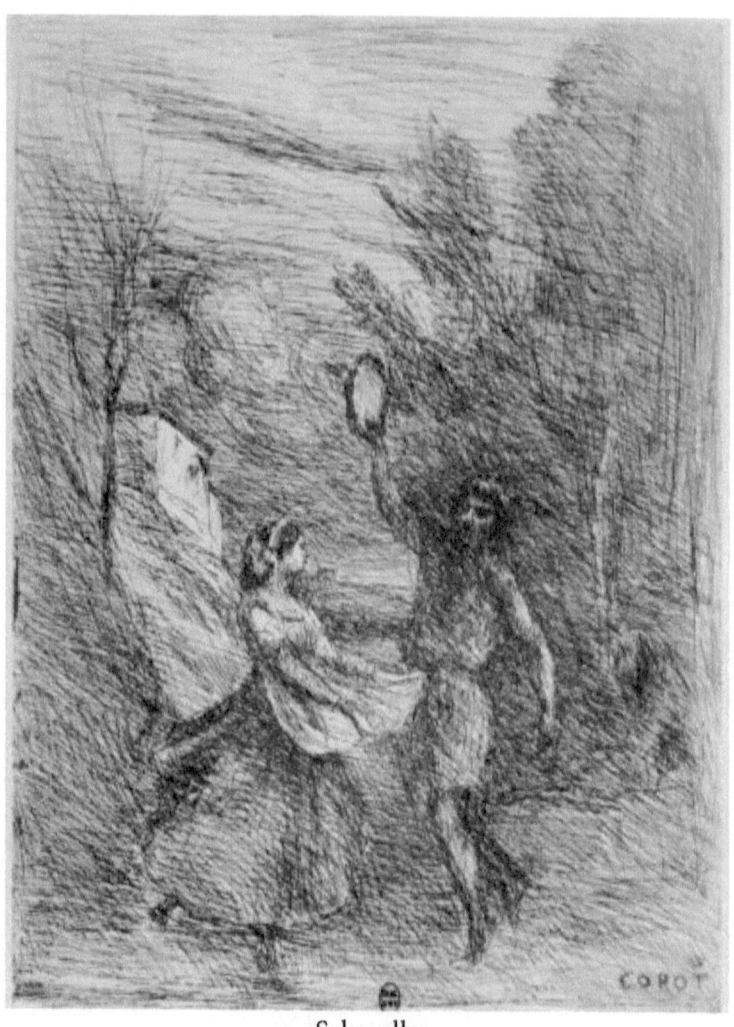

Saltarelle
1858, etching

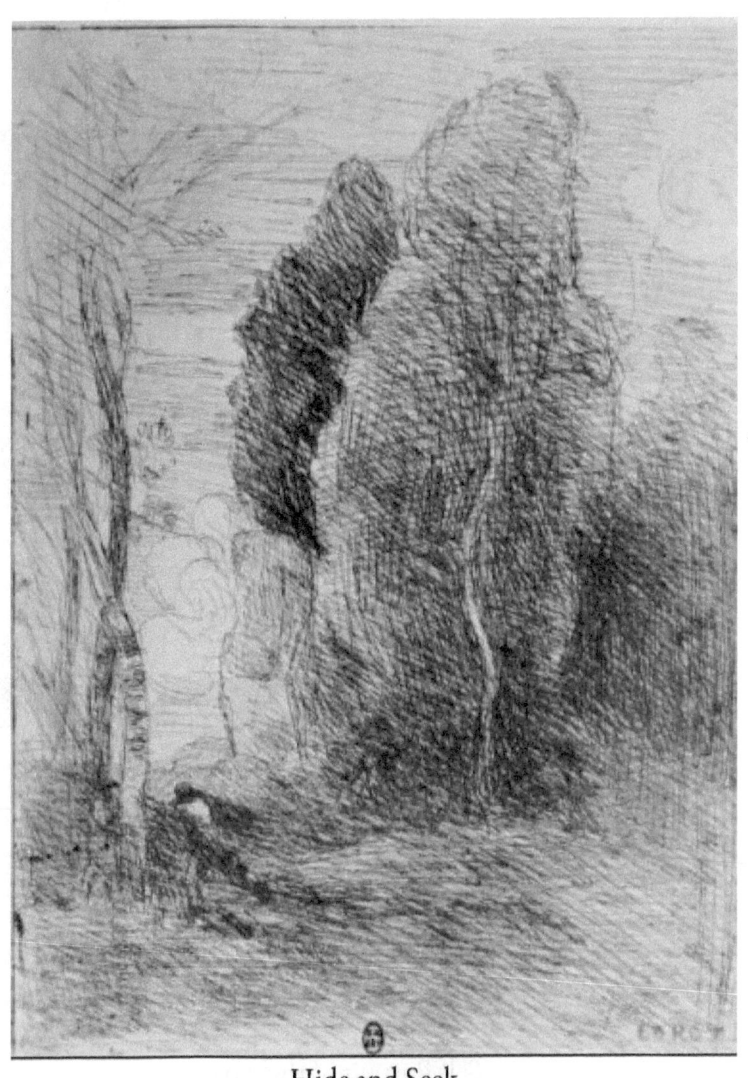

Hide and Seek
1858, etching

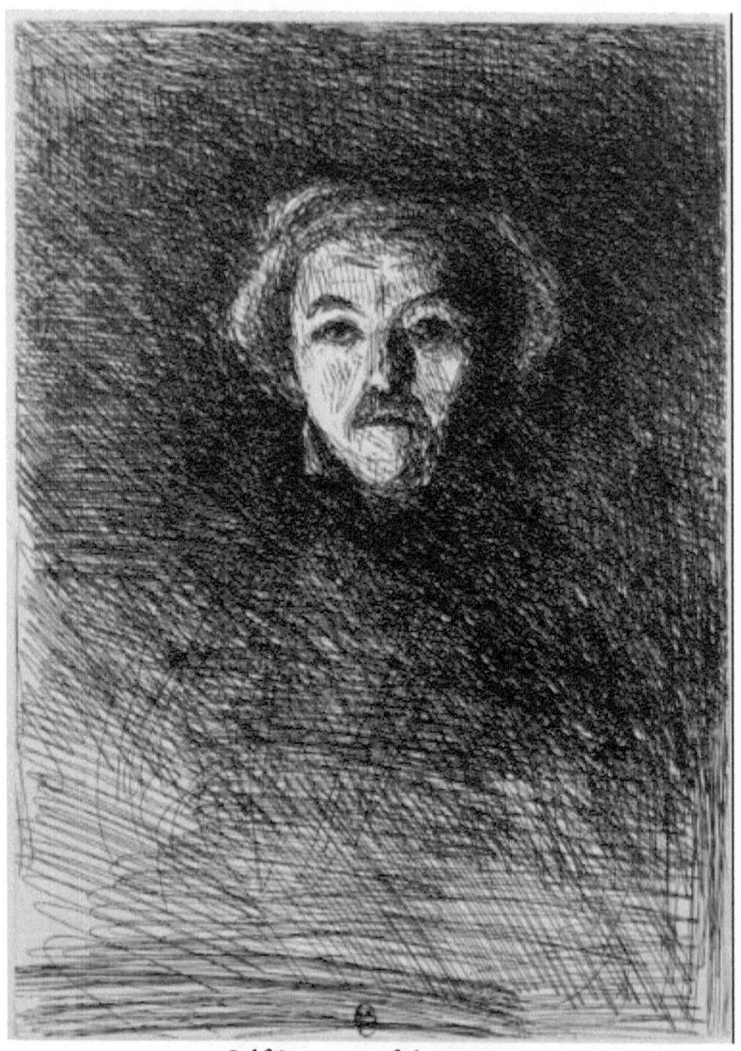

Self Portrait of the Artist
1858, etching

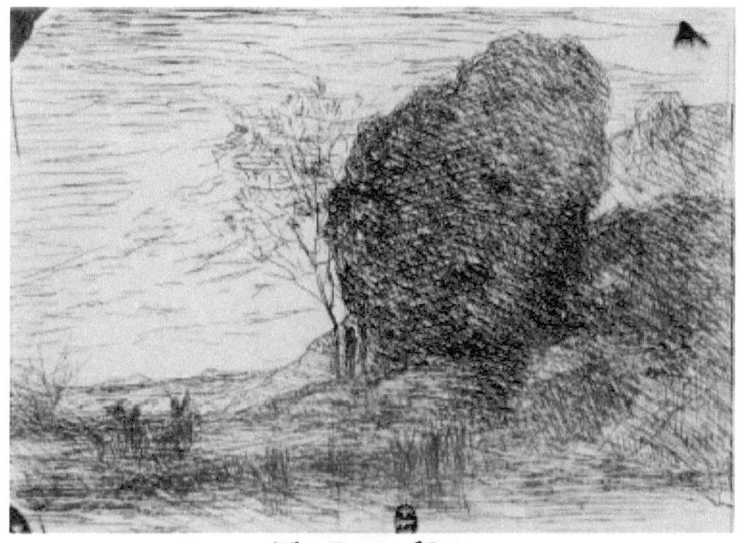

The Feast of Pan
1860, etching

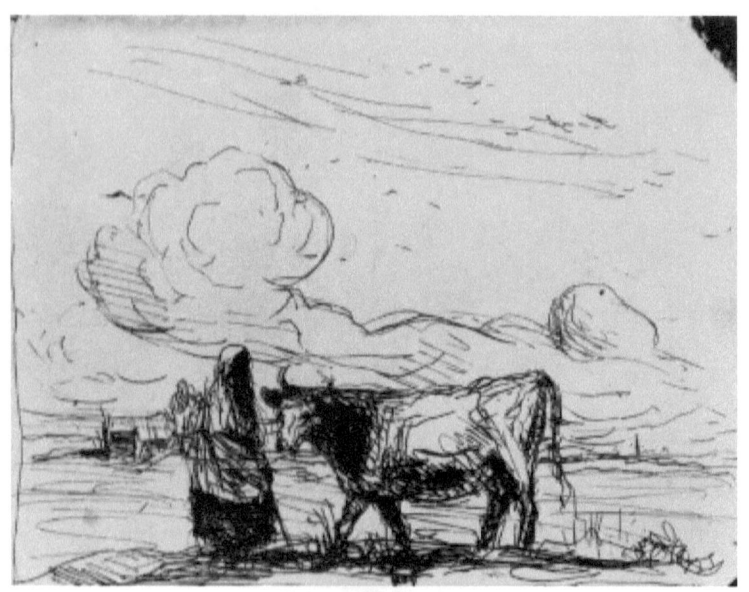

Cow with keeper
1860, etching

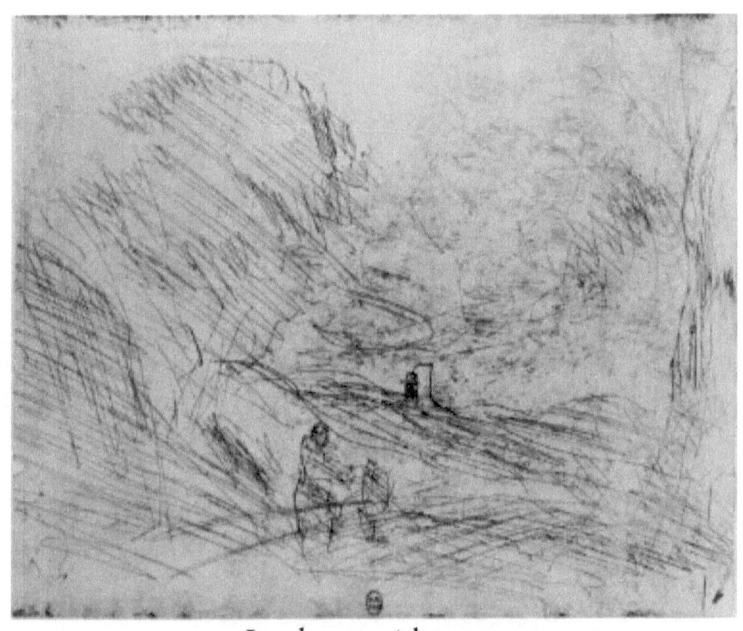

Landscape with tower
1860, etching

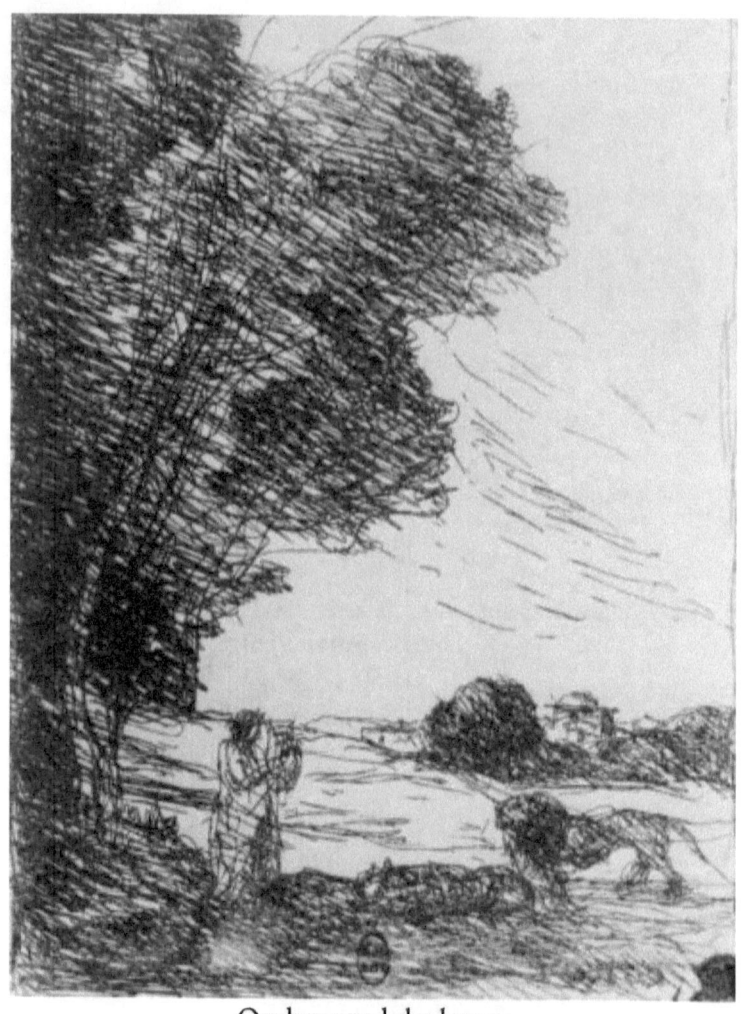

Orpheus and the beasts
1860, etching

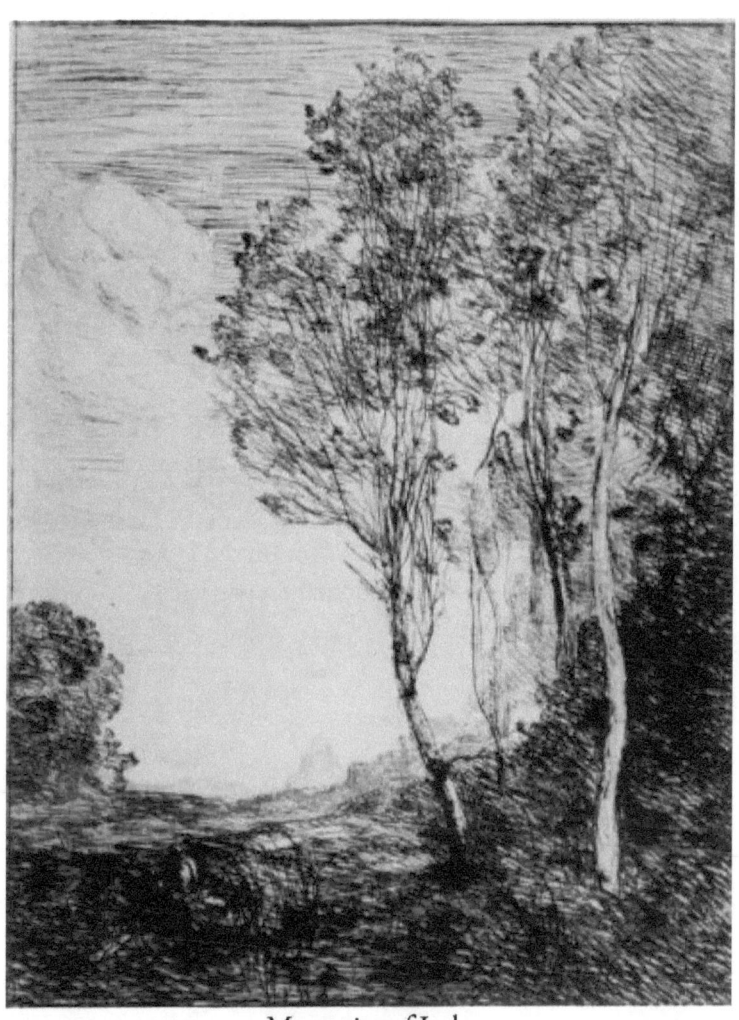

Memories of Italy
1863, etching

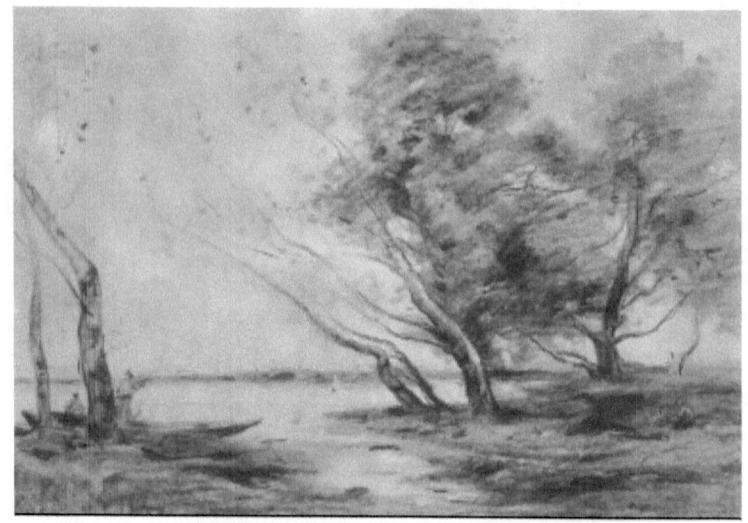

Landscape with Tree on the Lake
1865, Charcoal on paper

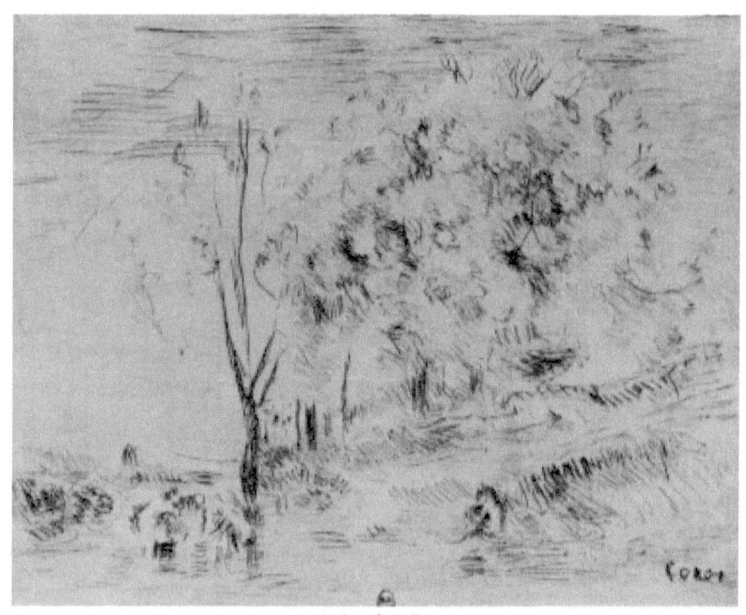

The bath
1865, etching

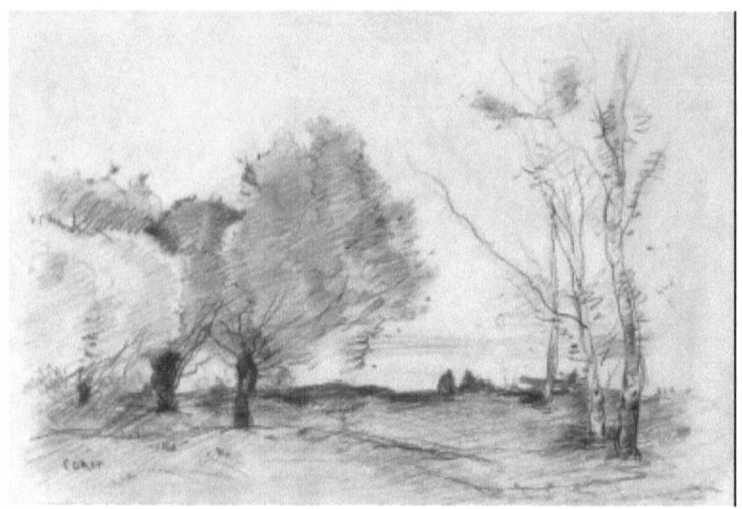

Willows and White Poplars
1865-1872, crayon and pencil on wove paper

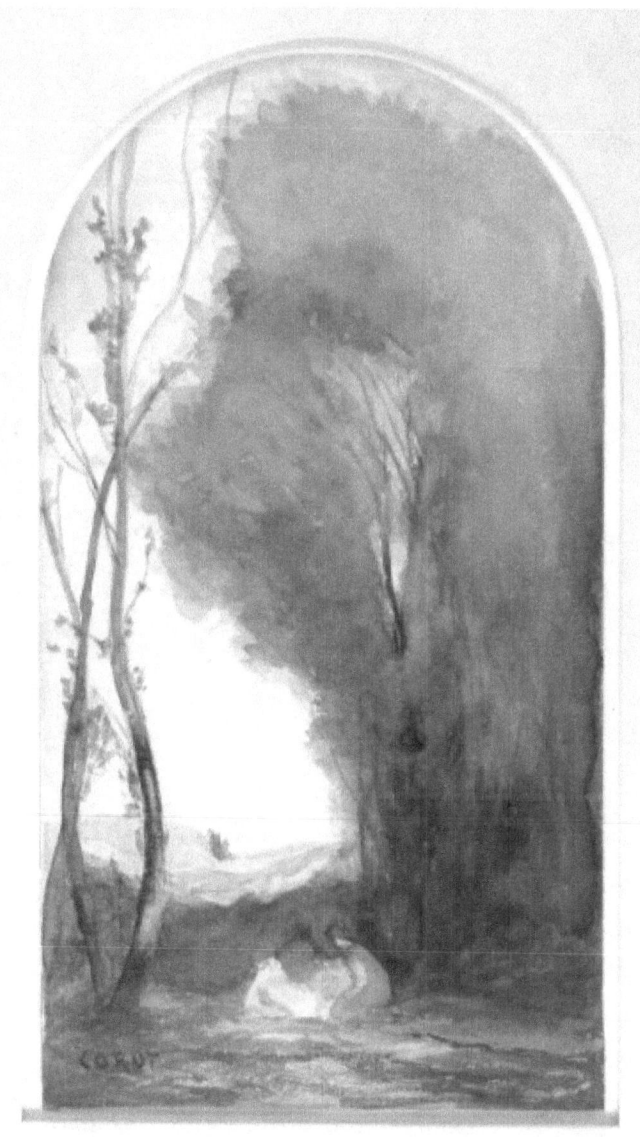

Study of Saint Sebastian
1867, watercolor and graphite underdrawing on cream,
moderately thick, slightly textured wove paper

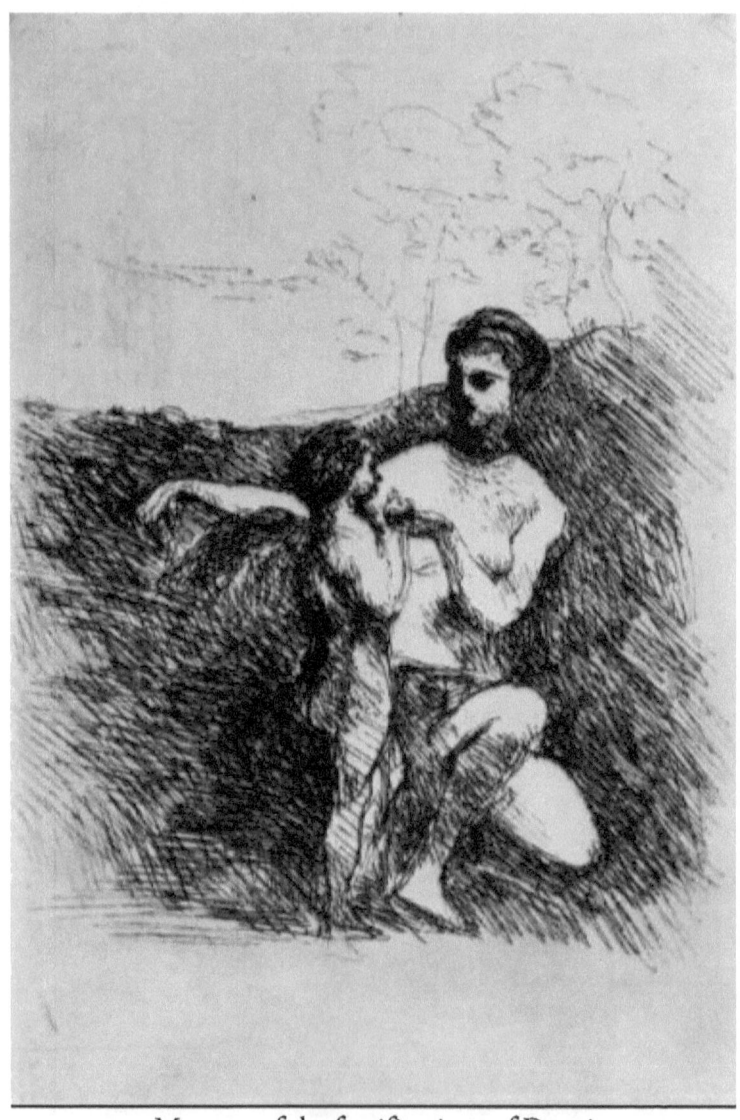

Memory of the fortifications of Douai
1869-70, etching

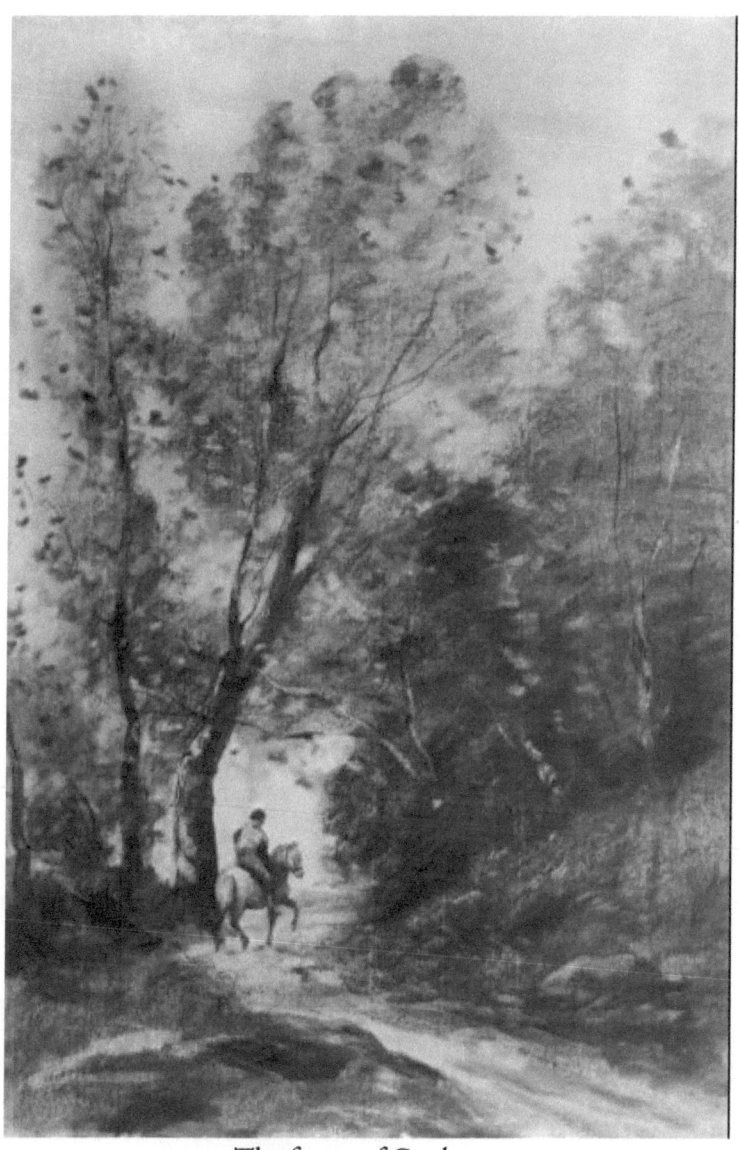

The forest of Coubron
1870, Charcoal on paper

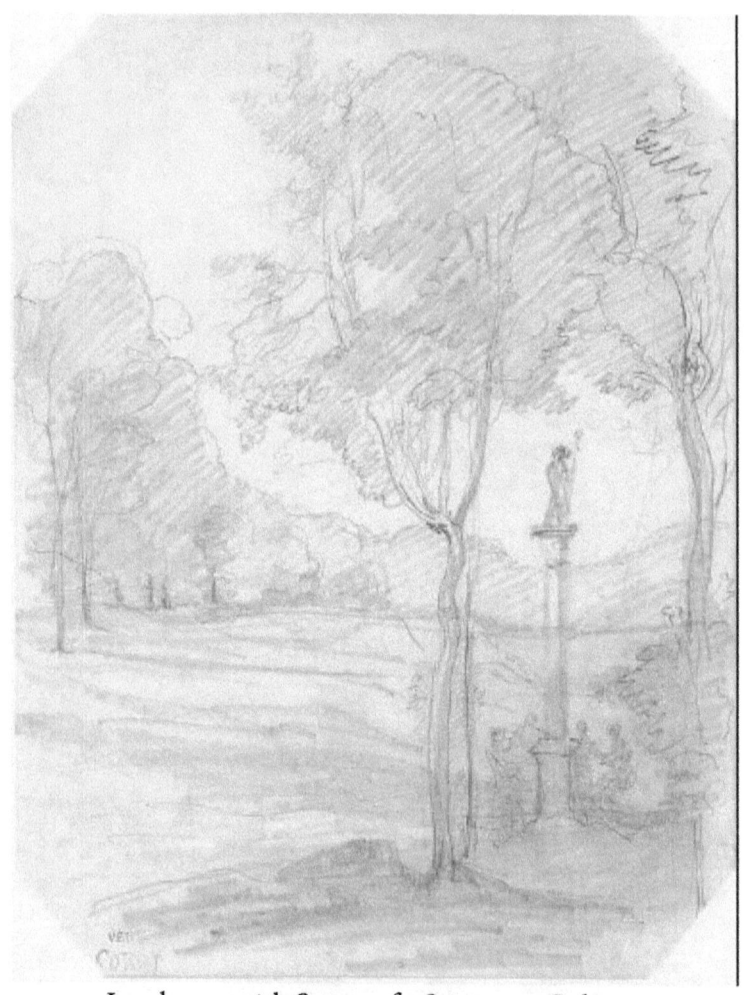

Landscape with Statue of a Saint on a Column
1870, pencil on paper

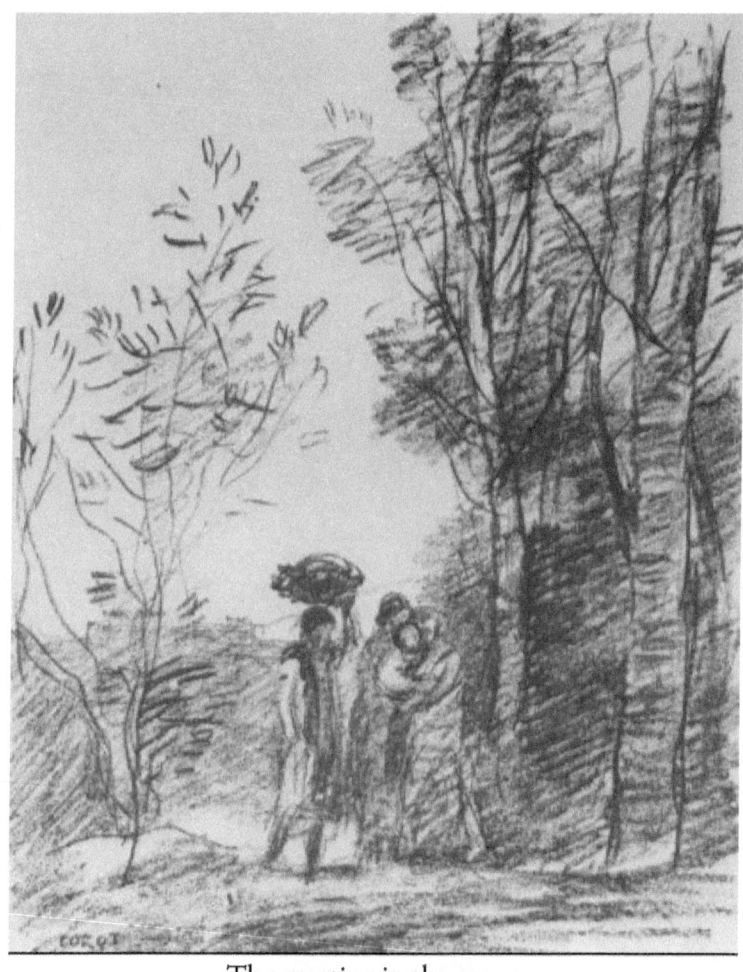

The meeting in the grove
1871, etching

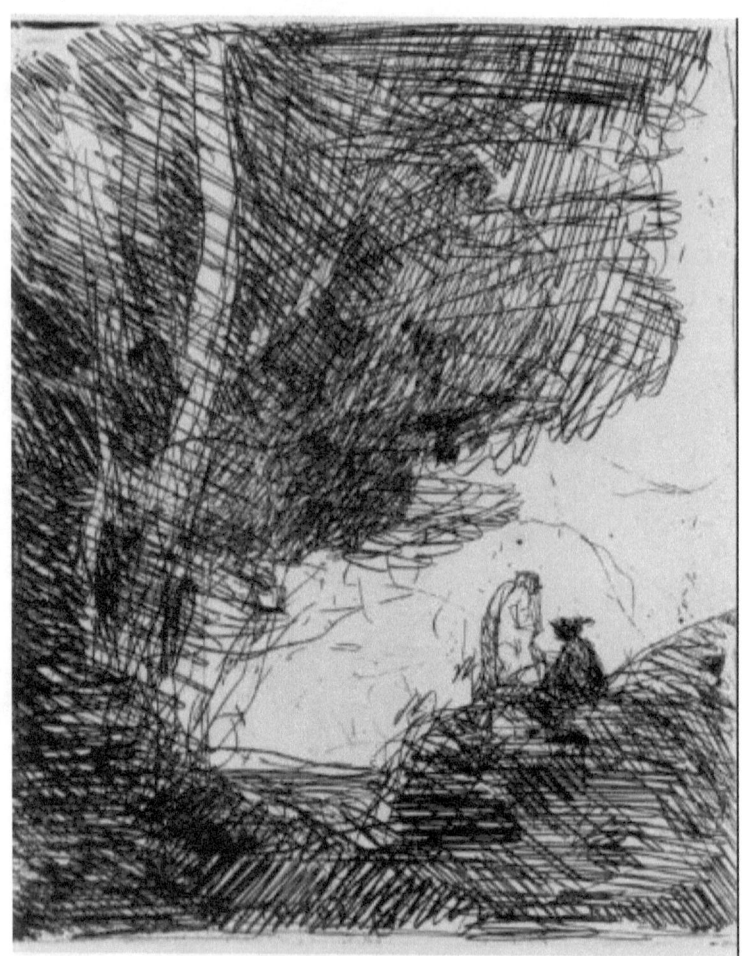

The poet and the muse
1871, etching

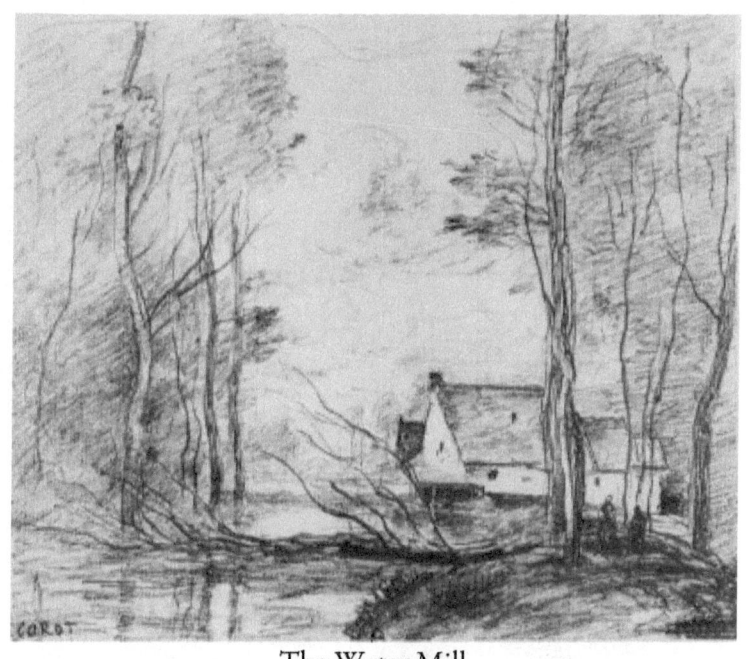

The Water Mill
1871, etching

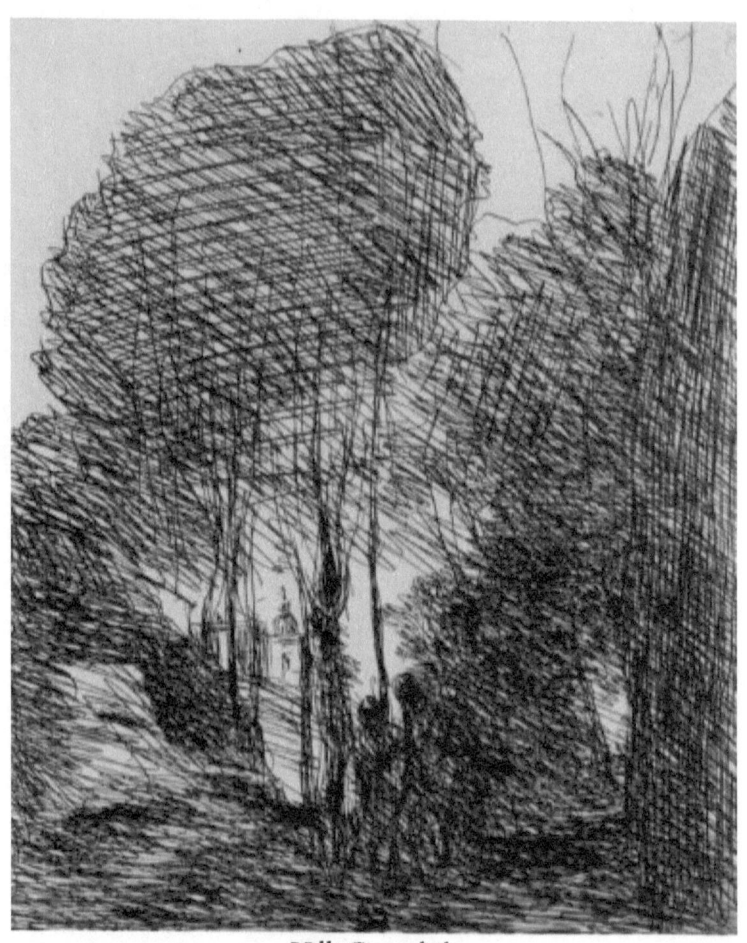

Villa Pamphili
1871, etching

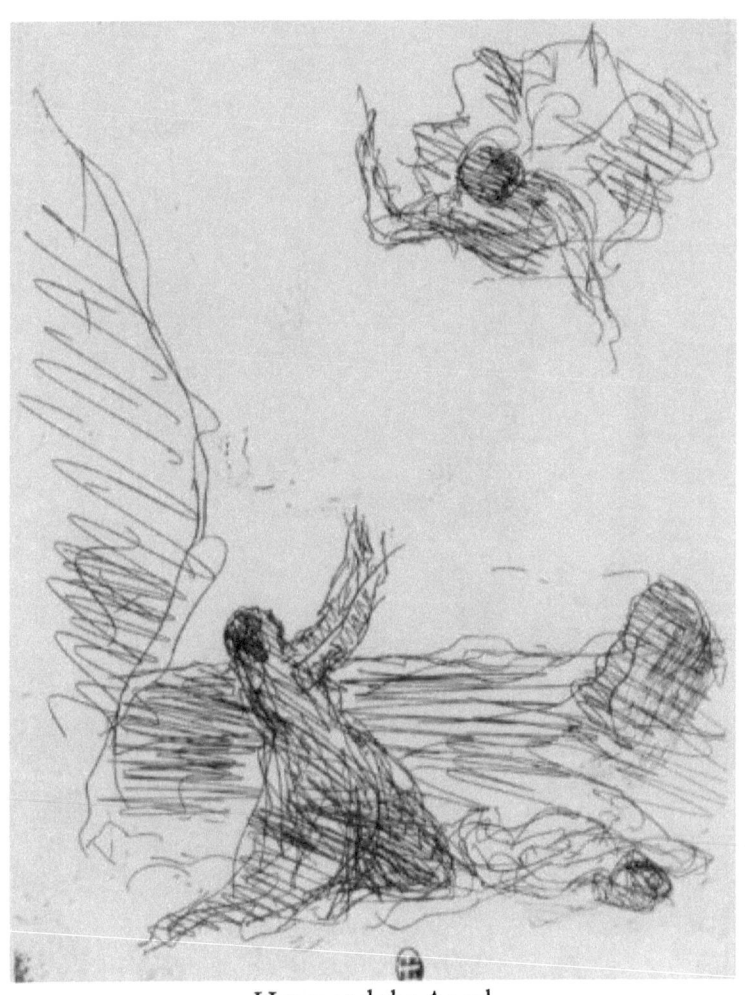

Hagar and the Angel
1871, etching

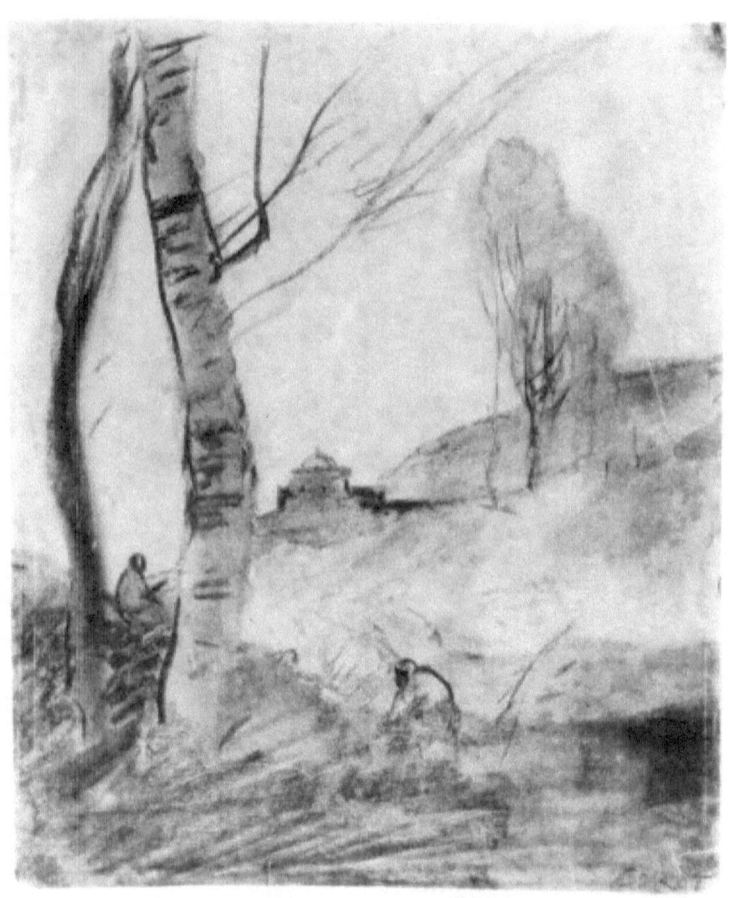

Memory of Ariccia
1871-72, Charcoal on paper

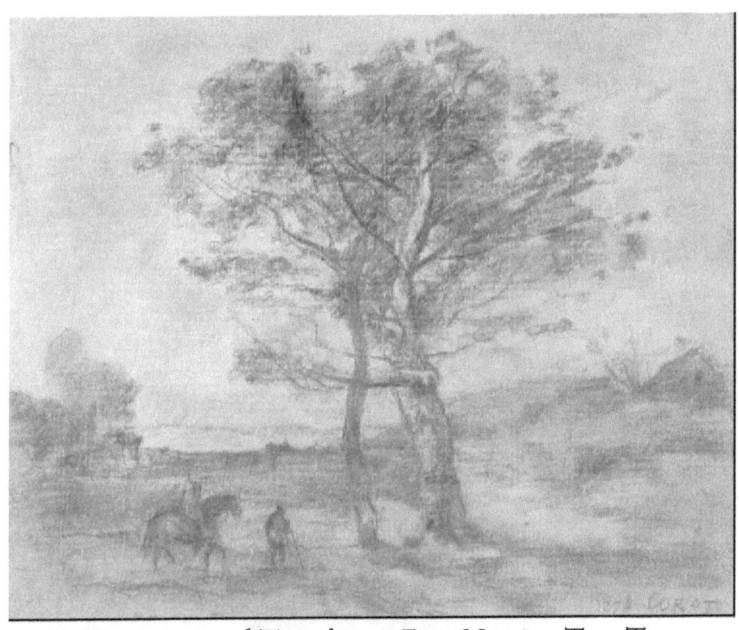

A Horseman and Traveler on Foot Nearing Two Trees
1874, charcoal and black chalk

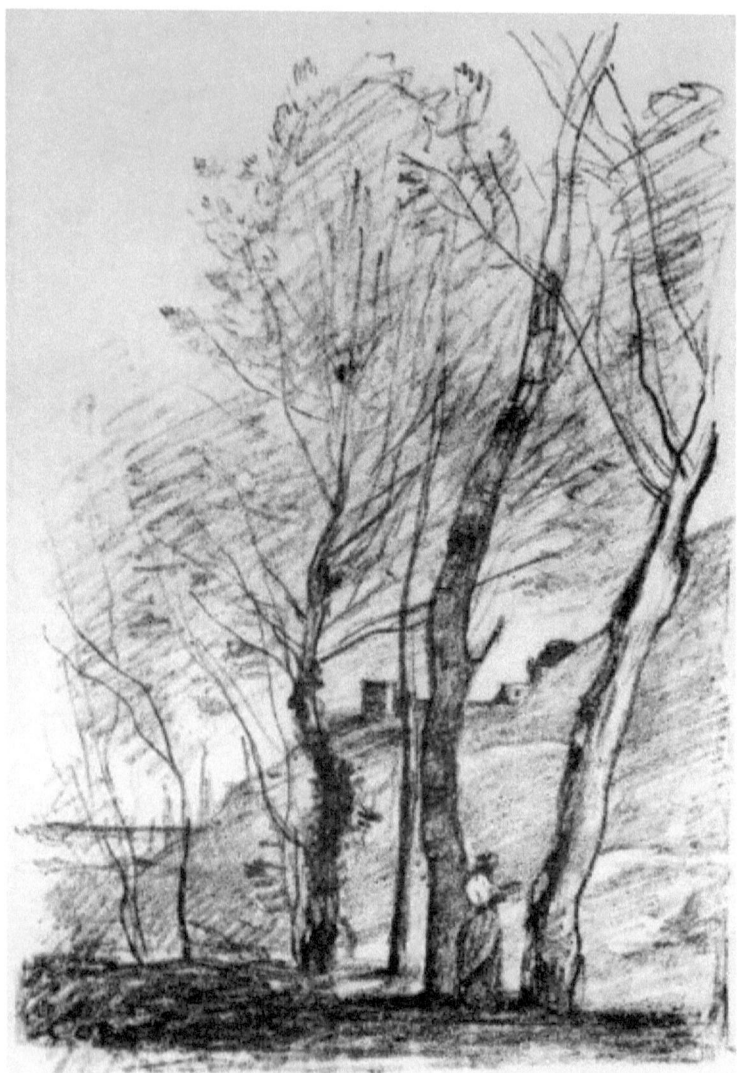

The reading under the trees
1874, etching

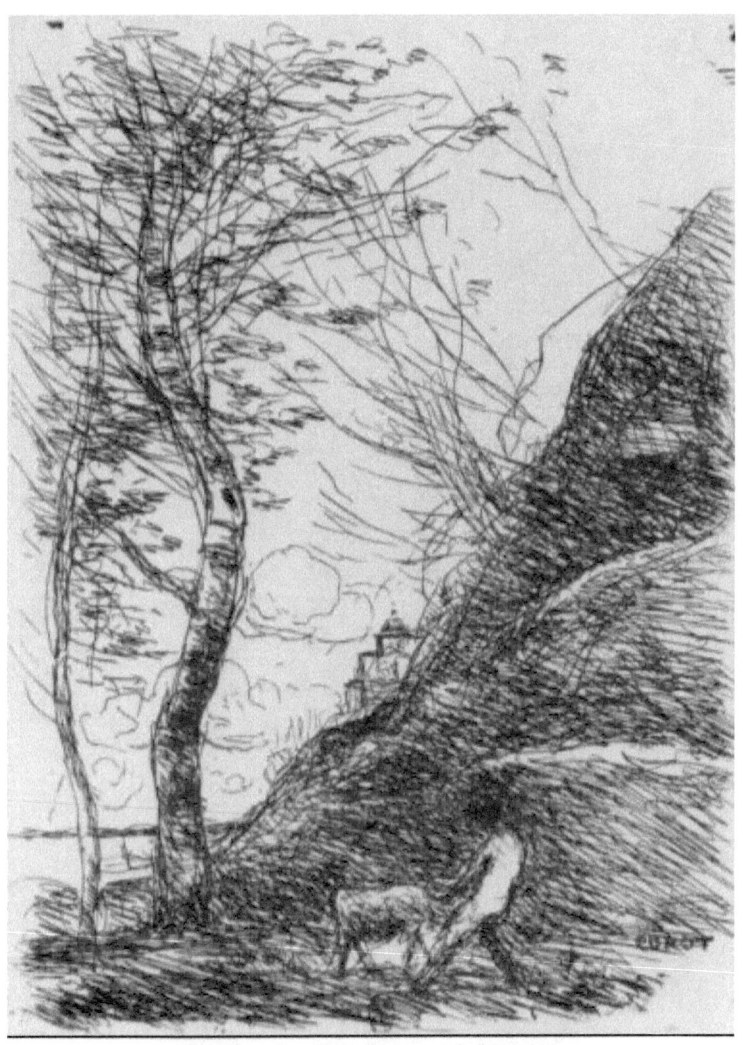

Shepherd, struggling with his goat
1874, etching

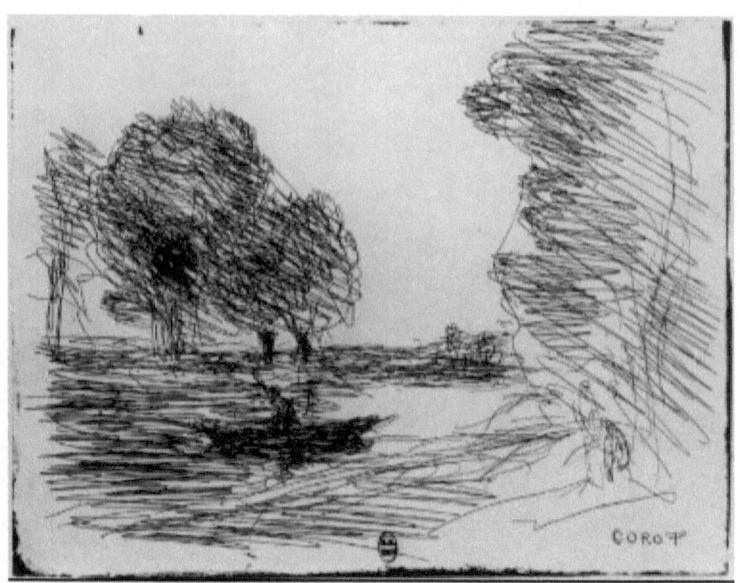

The boatman
1874, etching

Did you love *Camille Corot: 175 Paintings, Drawings and Etchings*? Then you should read *Artemisia Gentileschi: 52 Masterpieces* by Maria Tsaneva!

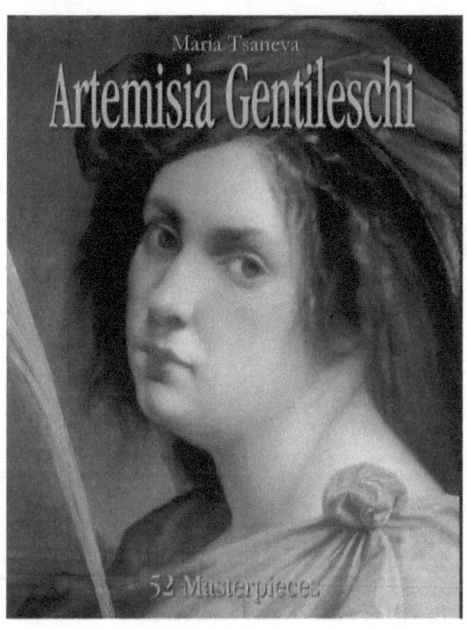

Artemisia Gentileschi was an Italian Baroque painter, considered one of the most accomplished painters in the generation following that of Caravaggio. In an era when women painters were not easily accepted by the artistic community or patrons, she was the first woman to become a member of the Accademia di Arte del Disegno in Florence. She painted many pictures of strong and suffering women from myth and the Bible - victims, suicides, warriors - and made it her specialty to paint the Judith story. Her best-known work is Judith Slaying Holofermes (a well-known medieval and baroque subject in art), which "shows the decapitation of

Holofernes, a scene of horrific struggle and blood-letting". That she was a woman painting in the seventeenth century and that she was raped and participated in prosecuting the rapist, long overshadowed her achievements as an artist. For many years she was regarded as a curiosity. Nowadays she is regarded as one of the most talented and expressionist painters of her generation.